I0418708

MY KID WANTS TO BE AN ACTOR!? NOW WHAT?

8 STEPS TO GETTING YOUR CHILD STARTED ON THE PATH TO A SUCCESSFUL ACTING CAREER

MAKEDA TENE' EKAKITIE

SHOWBIZ KIDS

CONTENTS

SHOWBIZ KIDS
8 STEPS ORGANIZER

A FREE GIFT TO OUR READERS
DOWNLOAD AT WWW.SHOWBIZ-KIDS.COM

PROLOGUE

Since I was a child, I have been an entertainer—singing, acting, dancing, piano, violin, writer —you name it. My life was a stage, and expressing myself creatively and artistically was second nature. I received early training at John S. Davidson Fine Arts Magnet School, The Augusta Mini Theatre, and The Augusta Ballet. I always compared my life at school to the movie *Fame*, where the kids would sing and dance in the hallways. Indeed, that was my reality. I would get up every morning, eager to go to school and be around like-minded kids who understood my passion for the arts. I could sashay down the hallways in the morning singing Diana Ross's "I'm Coming Out," settle in at lunch after singing one of my favorite Italian arias, "Pur di Cesti," and finish the day playing Beethoven's "Fur Elise" or coordinating my fingers in tune with any one of Bach's many intricate inventions. I enjoyed every minute of it!

When I was just a child, I begged my parents to take me to Los Angeles so I could pursue a professional career in acting. After all, I knew I could make it in Hollywood. However, my parents were working people with three children, and moving to Los Angeles for their child's career wasn't the priority. Don't get me wrong; my parents were terrific. They afforded me every opportunity to perform and hone my skills before I was old enough to make my move to "The Big City" after high school graduation. My mother produced yearly concerts for me as a teen: *Makeda Tene' in Concert*. Even while in college, my summer breaks included Mother producing magnificent concerts at Paine College, her alma mater, and I was able to sing, dance, and play piano to my heart's content. Mother was the OG of momagers and didn't even know it. She would ensure that all major press outlets were present at my concerts and proudly clipped the rave reviews from Augusta's finest newspapers, keeping them for my memories. And yes, I still have a copy of every single one of them.

My parents sent me on study trips to Spain and London so that I could gain exposure and knowledge of other cultures and use this connection in my passion for the arts. Shakespeare was always one of my favorite playwrights, and my parents were as thrilled as I was when I took photos sitting in front of his childhood home. They did their best to support my desires and aspirations. They even drove almost 2 hours to South Carolina twice a month so I could study with one of the most sought-after musical theatre vocal teachers who had been a Broadway star! This was before Zoom was invented, so everything had to be done in person. Although they couldn't uproot their lives to move to Los Angeles or New York City with me as a minor, my parents brought Hollywood to me and did their best to prepare me for that life. But I still wanted HOLLYWOOD despite the fantastic performing opportunities and "local celebrity status" I enjoyed in Augusta, GA.

I would tell my mom, "If I had a super talented child, I would move to Los Angeles if they wanted to be an actor and pursue their dreams!"

"Well, wait until you have a child, and you can do just that," she would say.

After high school, I moved to New York City for college. I performed off-Broadway and trained with Broadway and Metropolitan Opera vocal coaches. It was mind-blowing and exhilarating. Finally, I would get to live the life I desired and pursue my professional dreams. After college in NYC, I studied in Italy and toured with my mentor, vocal coach (now Global "Singing Lady" sensation), Cheryl Porter. The lessons I learned in those few months were life-changing. I am forever grateful for *Mama Cheryl's* mentorship. She was a big sister, confidant, and all-around fantastic human being in my life who boosted my performance confidence. I returned to the USA ready to take on several theatre tours and ultimately make the big move to HOLLYWOOD!

I arrived in Los Angeles, and the magic continued. I became a SAG actor, built my acting, writer, and producing resumes, and released my debut album, *In the Atmosphere*, which landed on the ballot of the 2018 Grammy Awards in 2 categories. I wrote a one-woman musical play, *Love in Concert*, a few years after arriving in Los Angeles, and it has been one of the most notable projects I've created and performed to date. I've been blessed to share this project with sold-out audiences in Los Angeles and my hometown of Augusta. And yes, Mother was the producer for the Augusta show, of course. Even though she couldn't bring me to Los Angeles before I turned 18, she instilled in me the importance of blooming where you are planted. Be excellent wherever you are and in whatever you do. And her most significant nugget of advice: "Don't ever wait for Hollywood to choose you. You choose yourself and create your own projects." From *Makeda Tene' in Concert* to *Love in Concert*, my self-written album, and now this book, I've taken Mother's advice—and it hasn't failed me yet.

When my son was born, I could tell he was pretty precocious, even as a newborn. Before he was born, I had a dream. He was born as a five-year-old. Nanny, my dearly beloved grandmother, was in the dream and told me that Innocent (my son) would be the family's game changer. She predicted that he would gain success at an accelerated rate. As a boy, I just knew my son understood what I was saying to him and that he could even understand my silly jokes. He would smirk and grin on cue. I remember sitting him on the bed while I would try out new songs on the piano and watch him for approval. He was an attentive audience and sat mesmerized. Of course, he couldn't move or go anywhere, but I also felt that he was really vibing to my music, y'all! He laughed, cried, and swayed to the rhythm. (Ok, maybe the crying part was because he needed a diaper change or some milk.) Still, he gave me so much positive "feedback" that I wondered what great things were in store for him. But what were the odds that he would want to act, sing, and dance through his life as I did? *Naaaah. Probably not.*

When Innocent was three, I could no longer deny it. His comedic timing, speech, and imitations were amazing! He would accompany me to singing gigs and watch his dad (a professional comedian) perform. He told me that he wanted to be on TV. I said, "Huh? You what?" And then the vow I made came crashing back to memory. "If I had a super talented kid, I would move to LA and let them follow their dreams." Well, I'm already in LA—check. What other excuse could I give? None. I knew what was in store for me. It wasn't an easy decision. I had heard that being the momager of a kid actor was INTENSE.

I'd even seen reality shows about the fierce competition between moms of kids on set. Was I ready for this? Was I willing to sacrifice certain aspects of my career to allow this little person, who could barely conjugate subjects and verbs correctly, to explore uncharted territory? Was I prepared to expand my learning curve from being an adult in the entertainment industry to navigating the challenging world of kids in the same industry? I had my answer when I looked into that tiny, perfectly round face. I saw him as a young boy practicing dance steps while watching his favorite Disney shows and belting out his favorite tunes. I watched in awe as that little one imitated his father's Nigerian accent and comedy and tried to sing my high notes after watching me on stage. I knew what I had to do. Hello. My name is Makeda. And I am a *Momager*.

INTRODUCTION

Get Ready for the Role of Your Life!

"My goal is to assist my child in developing a respectable and successful career in the entertainment industry and have a seamless transition into the world of an adult actor (if he so chooses)."

UrbanDictionary.com defines a momager as "a parent who pushes their child or children into show business at the risk of their mental and physical health and without any regard to their social development or privacy." First, allow me to take a moment to salute some of the most successful momagers and popagers for helping their children build lucrative and life-changing brands of global influence: Christopher Pearman (Raven-Symoné), Tina and Matthew Knowles (Beyoncé), and Kazembe Ajamu Coleman (Zendaya). These momagers and popagers, among others, have shown the world the positive impact a parent's guidance can have on their child's career.

I still remember that sunny day when the annual fair came to my hometown. I was standing with my parents, waiting for the entertainment to begin. A young Raven-Symoné walked by as her Dad led her through the crowd. She was getting ready to perform a song from her new album. I remember thinking how awesome it was that Raven's Dad played such a big part in her professional career. We all knew her from "The Cosby Show" and "That's So Raven."

We should all take notes. Of course, UrbanDictionary.com's definition is a tongue-in-cheek description and is highly subjective, depending on your point of view. Allow me to offer an alternative definition, which should encompass most of us who are in the position of having children in the entertainment industry.

> **Momager or Popager:** A parent who encourages, supports, and protects their child or children while navigating the world of show business. They consider their child's overall mental, emotional, social, and physical health. These parents pay close attention to and encourage positive social development as their children grow into healthy young adults and productive members of society.

That sounds much better. We should all strive to be this type of Showbiz Parent.

Before starting this business, you must define and know your goal. **My goal is to assist my child in developing a respectable and successful career in the entertainment industry and transitioning seamlessly into the world of an adult actor (if he so chooses).** I'm not about making waves and getting a bad reputation in this industry because, as the saying goes, "People talk." This industry talks. And industry talk can lead your child down a path of rejection simply because the word around town is "Johnny's parents are dramatic and hard to work with." Don't be *that* parent!

I can't stress enough the importance of mentally and emotionally preparing to support your child's career in the acting business. This step is CRUCIAL. Even before I left home for college, one of my goals (other than becoming a professional in the industry) was to get a degree in psychology to help myself, my colleagues, and others deal with this infamous industry. I decided to get my Master's Degree in Clinical Psychology to understand the psychology and personalities behind this exclusive "Hollywood world." I wanted to be prepared to help myself and my fellow actors deal with the inevitable insecurities, rejection, self-doubt, and struggles that come with this territory. One thing that works for me is ensuring my son stays grounded, knows his worth, understands his value, and understands that no human being is the holder of his destiny. However you decide to do this as a parent, it must be done.

I bolster my son daily with affirmations, and he has now begun to say them on his own. (The younger we start, the easier it sticks.) My son was three years old when he started his professional career. I don't know what goes on in that 8-year-old brain now, but I can tell you that Innocent thinks he's the best thing since Nutella and sliced bread. Can I pinpoint a specific moment that he adopted this mentality? No. Why? Because it was an ongoing conscious effort from the start to ensure he knows his worth is not tied to a job. His worth is not linked to whether or not a director appears to favor one child on set over the other. His self-worth comes from within; it comes from having a solid community around him that validates him with unconditional positive regard.

My belief in God has helped me maintain balance and stability in this industry. Whatever spiritual belief you subscribe to, I believe it is essential to share that with your child. Whatever has helped you "do life" and gotten you to the point where you're still standing and standing tall, impart this to your children. Believe it or not, they are listening. I remember when we met with a well-known agency in Beverly Hills. We approached this unique high-rise building and were met by security dressed in official black suits. "What's your name, and who are you here to see?" one of the guys asked in his most professional voice.

"Innocent Ekakitie, here for …."

The man nodded, made a phone call, and spoke the name *Innocent Ekakitie*. He looked back at us, nodded, and motioned for us to approach another exclusive elevator where we were granted access to a particular floor. Innocent's dad and I looked at each other with silent amazement. Wow, our 5-year-old was taking us places. For some reason, the theme song from *The Jeffersons* by Janet Dubois and Jeff Barry kept playing in my head. When it was time, the agent came out to greet us. Innocent was sitting with great confidence because he had never been taught to be nervous, and, generally speaking, he does not have the spirit of fear. The agent asked if she could talk to him alone for a few moments, and then we would be brought in.

I was nervous. *How will my baby represent himself well without mama bear next to him?* As Dad and I waited outside, we exchanged looks again. This time, they were unspoken glances. *Uh oh, what is this child going to say? I hope he doesn't say the wrong thing!* When we entered the room, we found our little boy sitting confidently in one of the black swivel chairs at the head of a long conference table. He was beaming and all smiles. I waited anxiously as we all watched him enjoying his merry-go-round chair. The agent finally spoke. "He's so confident. He told me about his

Sabbath School class and how he learned about the Good Samaritan," she said smiling. *Whew! Good boy!* That experience was a confidence booster; I knew Innocent would be able to hold his own in this industry.

The average person would have felt intimidated in such an environment, perhaps feeling like their destiny rested on the shoulders of the "all-knowing agent." How do I know? I used to feel this same way when I started my journey. Agents and those in high places in this industry seemed almost superhuman to me, and I would feel nervous, praying that they would like me and choose me for the part. Not my little pumpkin! It didn't matter to him. He entered the room assuming he would be well received and had no concept of anything different. Parents, this is an advantage our children have. The innocence of childhood is priceless. Don't take anything personally, even if it is. Long story short, my son's confidence and spiritual grounding secured him an "across the board" offer that day, even though we only sought representation in one area. The contracts were drawn up before we left the room. We decided to pass on that offer, but that experience was just another stone in a solid foundation.

Being an active participant in your child's career is a sacrifice. It's a sacrifice that you must be willing and able to embrace. Keeping your child balanced and grounded will be a challenge if you're not grounded and balanced. And believe me, they will need your guidance in this area. No acting coach or teacher can fill this position for you. Building a solid support community around you and your child is crucial. You can't take advice from every source. It's like building an invisible fortress of protection around you and your family as you go through this business. There will be those you trust inside and outside the industry with whom you trust to speak words over your situation. Allowing everyone to share their opinions could disorganize and discourage you.

Once you decide to go all the way, follow through. Some will say, "Why are you letting your child work? Just let them be a kid." Well, that's all fine and dandy, but they don't know your child, and they don't know your situation. I can go all-in with my son because I know what it feels like to want something so badly at an early age, and all you need is that adult figure in your life to help you reach that next level. Not every child has career-driven passions early in life, but many do, and these children can change the world. Suppose Wolfgang Amadeus Mozart's father denied him the opportunity to make music at the tender age of four. In that case, we might not have some of my favorite musical masterpieces to date. He began composing at age five and was engaged as a musician at the Salzburg court by age 17. His sister was also a child prodigy who began studying the harpsichord at seven and started touring with her brother. Both children had passions for music, and their father personally encouraged, taught, and instructed their musical careers. Popager Mozart took an active role. Perhaps the person questioning you has never encountered children who can articulate their purpose and goals early.

Personally, I find it an honor to work with these youths. Acting is a craft and a gift, just like musical ability. I could assure you that no one would dissuade you if your child sat down to play a moving Rachmaninoff concerto at age seven with the Chicago Symphony Orchestra. Absolutely not! They would praise you for being such a great parent supporting your prodigy's dreams and goals. Acting should be no different. Talent is talent. And it should all be encouraged and supported.

Before we get to the veggie meat and potatoes, allow me to add this critical piece of advice. Even though this may be your child's desire and dream, check in with them periodically to ask how they're feeling. Are they enjoying the process? Always remember that this is about your child, not you. A parent should never push their child into this industry to live vicariously or fulfill their dreams of gaining stardom. One thing that sold me about hiring Innocent's manager is that she expressed those same sentiments. If your child begins to exhibit dysfunction and no longer desires to be in the entertainment business, it is time to reassess.

Innocent will tell you that I check in with him often. "Baby, are you happy? Do you love this?"

Even when the pressure of auditions and shooting projects gets intense, he tells me, "Yes, I'm good. I still want to do this for life. I'll let you know if that changes, Mom."

"OK, baby … deal."

STEP ONE

THE WINNING HEADSHOT

"For your child actor, a headshot should accurately represent your child physically and show off their extraordinary personality."

Back in the day, everyone gave out their business cards or "calling cards." Remember those? It ensured that the person you had just met didn't forget about you and could have something to refer to quickly if they ever wanted to contact you. If you were like me, I was always impressed by the business cards that looked like the owner spent time, effort, and resources making them look amazing. The cards that looked done on a home printer, with ruffled edges ripped off, did not make the best impression. If I put two cards side by side for the same service, I will likely call the company that looks the most professional and polished. For an actor, headshots are the calling card. **For your child actor, a headshot should accurately represent your child physically and show off their extraordinary personality.**

The photos are crucial to getting your child in the door. Managers, agents, casting directors, and producers are all interested in finding out, "Who is the little girl behind the Colgate smile that can light up the room?" Or "Who is this little boy with the mischievous grin and the sparkling eyes?" A great headshot should spark interest. It should nudge the viewer to want to learn more, see more, and ultimately meet the face in this great headshot in person. People advise young actors, "The headshots don't matter. Just get a couple of good shots on your phone and send them in."

You can do this if you like. But today, there's no room for mediocrity in the entertainment industry. The only time this works is for babies. There's no real reason to get professional shots for this age group because their looks change weekly. Still, some parents are going the extra mile to get professional photos for even the newest addition to their family. Why? Because they understand that presenting the highest quality and best version of their child is essential. In this business, there's always someone else out there who is willing to do whatever it takes to help their child STAND OUT from the crowd. Set a precedent for your child actor and realize that investing in them is worth it because your child is worth it.

Hard copy photos with resumes stapled to the back used to be the norm. Agents and casting directors would go through stacks of pictures and separate them into "trash" or "keep" piles without even reading the resume. How could someone be that insensitive? Don't they want to at least acknowledge those cute little faces before throwing them away with last night's Thai takeout? No. Why? Because time is money, and they don't have time to waste. I saw it for myself when I interned at a youth management company. Dozens of submissions would come in every day. When I got to work, I saw many beautiful little kids' photos in the trash before 9 am. It broke my heart! That's somebody's baby! How could they? When I asked the managers, they would simply say they don't waste time if the headshot doesn't grab them at first glance because a hundred more will come in before the end of the week.

That was many years ago. Is that still true today? Even now, a dear manager friend of mine still does the same thing with the electronic submissions that come through the computer. If the headshot is weak, they skip it. Even if they glance at the resume, the first impression is the lasting impression. "If they don't even care enough to get a good headshot, I don't want to work with them," this manager would always say.

I got Innocent's first headshots when he was just three years old. I was accustomed to having my headshots done as an adult, but there are some specific things

I've learned when taking kids' headshots. I didn't have a guide to help me maneuver the whole kid industry thing, so I learned as I went along. Finding the right photographer who has experience taking children's headshots or one who is open and patient enough to take these headshots is crucial.

FINDING THE RIGHT PHOTOGRAPHER

Unless you want to, I don't recommend spending hundreds of dollars on the first headshot session, especially if your child is under six. At this age, kids' features change so much that I used to schedule a session every six months just to keep up with Innocent's changing look. One month he has a mouth full of teeth, and the next, his two front teeth are missing. The following six months, they've grown again, so you've got to keep up and ensure each photo represents your child's current appearance. For example, Casting is looking for a boy with two front teeth missing. They see your child's headshot in the system (from six months ago) and call him in for an audition. When he comes in, they are greeted by a smiling kid with completely grown-in adult teeth in front. *Uh, oh.*

Choosing a great photographer for your child can be pretty straightforward. You can start by word of mouth and asking friends who may have kids in the industry to give you referrals. If not, you can start by doing a google search for photographers in your area, and make sure you check their Kids Headshot section. Do the photos "pop?" Can you almost imagine the type of personality that kid in the picture has in real life? Does the photographer have complimentary reviews? When you speak to them over the phone, are they patient in answering your questions? In this world of Instagram, finding a good photographer can be elementary, and you can quickly see their work and reviews (look under the comments section) all in one place!

I don't quite remember how I found Innocent's first photographer, but I hit a goldmine when I did. Angel Bousquet was a young man from Puerto Rico wearing a black leather jacket, beard, and boots. I would have never guessed that he had such experience taking children's headshots, but he knew how to instruct Innocent and get that "perfect" shot. At one point, Innocent wanted to get creative and asked if he could take pictures pretending to be a ninja, running with all his might. My motherly instinct wanted to dismiss that idea and bring my child's focus back to reality. Instead, Angel quietly said to him, "Ok, we'll do that pose right after we finish this set." Instantly, Innocent was cooperative. Angel validated my son's creative ideas and returned him to the task. When it was time for Innocent to do his fun shots, he was encouraged and so happy! Those running ninja photos were some of the session's best and most natural images. Innocent felt free to express himself and participate in the process, which yielded some of the most honest and engaging photos. Even if you don't end up professionally using any of those ninja-type shots, let your child be an active participant in what's going on. They will take more pride in their photo session and be more open to taking direction if they feel respected and validated.

PREPARING FOR THE SESSION

The "Look"

In the industry, professionals often use the term "look" to refer to the different categories of photographs. There are generally two types of headshots, although there are several subcategories within each. For your child actor, we will focus on the main two.

A Commercial Look

A photo used mainly for commercial submissions is considered a commercial look. Nice, happy smiles are the focus of these shots. Whatever the advertisers want to sell, they will choose an actor who appears approachable, likable, confident, and joyful—all great qualities that can drive product sales. You can have more than one look in each category.

Each look can portray a distinct persona. For example, your 7-year-old may do a basic commercial look to represent a sporty kid with a jean jacket and t-shirt and another look to represent a school kid wearing glasses and a cardigan sweater. The retail industry is looking for kids who can sell their products, be a positive representative of their brand, and have a relatable feel. For commercials, it is best to use vibrant and bright colors to compliment your child's skin tone. Blues, greens, and purple tones perfectly complement Innocent's caramel complexion. Combined with his bright light-up-the-room smile, we always have many great commercial shots to choose from after his sessions. For the beginner, focusing on having a fabulous commercial shot is essential. Most kids will begin with commercial representation. Agents don't generally offer theatrical contracts to very young children unless they know your child has the acting chops from the beginning. But if your child is barely talking, the submissions will be more commercial and print (i.e., model/photography).

A Theatrical Look

This look is geared toward theatrical submissions, i.e., TV and film. Smiling is not as necessary for these shots, although you can add a few smiles here and there. The main goal is to convey a mood or intensity. For example, in Innocent's latest headshot session with Matt Stasi, we focused more on getting theatrical looks because he was getting more auditions for TV shows and film projects. The color palette was burgundy, blues, and darker greens, and the background mirrored this feeling with browns, maroon, and grays. Innocent would look intently at the camera or give a little bad boy smirk, and the photos turned out phenomenal! I was in awe when I saw the final shots. *Wow, is that my sweet baby boy?* He had become so many different characters in that one shoot!

Of course, we were able to get some commercial shots by switching up the clothing, background lighting, and focusing on that winning smile! You can tone down the bright colors for theatrical photos and explore darker shades to compliment your child's complexion. Choose appropriate clothing for your child's age group and the look you're going for. To save time, you can layer. For example, you may bring a solid color shirt and a jean jacket. Take pictures with the shirt first and then both the jacket and shirt. Make the wardrobe changes simple. The goal is to focus on your child's face and accentuate their features.

Hair and Makeup

In mentoring parents, I'm often asked, "How should I do their hair?" Hair is vital, especially for children with more naturally textured hair. I recently assisted a parent in signing her daughter with a talent agent. She needed to do headshots first, so I had her shoot with Angel. She sent me a picture of her 4-year-old's hair in long braids with synthetic hair extensions. When I first glanced at the picture, I thought *I'd love to see a picture of her natural hair.* When I requested the photo from her mother, it was a no-brainer. Her natural hair was shorter with a curly texture and framed her face perfectly, bringing out her natural beauty. Upon my advice, her mother took out the long braids, and the natural hairstyle was ready for the photo shoot the next day. The pictures were glorious! She signed with a manager a few weeks later.

Take about 20 minutes to watch commercials. You will find that most actors wear their naturally textured hair, or at least something similar. Go for the most natural look, especially with children. Your child can wear different hairstyles aside from their natural texture, but make sure whatever style you choose looks healthy and wholesome for their age.

Young children don't typically need much make-up. You can use skin-colored or translucent powder to eliminate the shine from the pictures, but no heavy foundation is necessary. I only use a nude lip gloss for Innocent to keep his lips moist and prevent the ashy look. For the entire three months Innocent was in Vancouver filming the *Ivy+ Bean* film series, the only thing they put on him was lotion (upon my request), sunscreen, and a lip balm. He got a tiny scratch on his forehead, which was lighter than the rest of his skin. I requested they add a little make-up to that area because he felt like it stood out (it didn't). Ten seconds later, they were done. Voila ... off to set he went! If big Hollywood sets aren't using much makeup on children, why should you do it in the headshot session? Less is more. If any skin smoothing is needed, your photographer will add a couple of edited photos to the package. Or you can do it yourself; it's a quick one-step process on a photo editing app! (*wink*). Let your child's natural beauty shine through. They don't need all that "extra" to be fabulous.

Set a Time Limit.

Facts: According to developmental psychologists (shout out to my fellow psychology majors!), a child's attention span can be safely calculated by multiplying their age by 2-3 minutes (Gobbell, 2020). For example, by the time Innocent was three and had his first headshot session, his attention span might be 6-9 minutes. At eight years old, he could manage 16-24 minutes. Know your child's patterns, set time limits, and be flexible. The goal is to capture the best personality and mood of your child. If you know your little one can only stay focused for ten minutes at a time, and you need to capture several looks, make sure to factor in a couple of breaks. A photographer should understand and plan according to your needs. Give them a heads-up during the preliminary planning stages of your shoot. Communication is key! For example, let the photographer know if your child has issues looking into bright lights. If your child doesn't like being outdoors, make sure you choose a photographer with studio options. It's better to be upfront rather than get to the shoot and spend unnecessary time, energy, and money, without getting the desired outcome.

Remove Distractions

Please leave all iPads, devices, and games at home. There's not much time, so this is one way to eliminate distractions that can become problematic during a session. If your child needs to take a break during a session, giving them the iPhone to watch YouTube or allowing them to hop on their favorite game isn't wise. They can still focus on the task at hand while taking a break. Perhaps the break is getting a drink or doing a fun dance move or exercise to rejuvenate their mind, body, and spirit. If you're taking shots outside, you can take a quick walk and enjoy the fresh air. Parents, it might be helpful to turn off your phones as well. This way, you're letting your child and the photographer know you are giving your undivided attention to the photo shoot. *Distracted parents equal distracted children.* I can't tell you how many times Innocent's focus shifts to me when he realizes I'm not fully present in the moment. Children are validated by their parents' attention or lack thereof. Support in every way, even during a headshot session, is crucial.

I also find it uplifting to have music playing. Photographers usually have various playlists on hand, or you can bring some suggestions. Whatever helps get your child focused and in the proper mindset to knock out those winning shots!

When Innocent was very young, we did many sessions outdoors. He was distracted by people walking by or making comments. Although the compliments and attention were sweet, they were distracting. I suggest finding a less crowded area for kids if you do an outdoor shoot. Remember, studio sessions have more controlled settings for minimizing distractions.

CHOOSING THE WINNING HEADSHOT

If you are entirely new to this industry, please take the photographer's advice. Let them know that you are new to the game and would like them to send their top choices for a commercial and a theatrical shot. Their experience should allow them to make decisions quickly. Also, check out their websites and other successful photographers' websites. They should have a section for kids, with the subtitles "Commercial" and "Theatrical." Study the poses and the types of shots featured on their website to assist you in making your choice.

If you understand headshot selections and have some experience in this area, look at the proofs when you get them from the photographer. Don't worry about making a selection the first go-round. When you give them a second look, jot down which photos catch your eye and continue to narrow them down until you select the top three in each category. Make sure you review the entire batch of images at least once before making any decisions.

When I initially received Innocent's first headshot session proofs, I found myself going through the batch and jotting down dozens of photo numbers. It's not easy to select one because this is your baby, and you think every photo of them is cute! You should go through them once with your Mama / Daddy eyes. The second look through, think as a professional—as if you're seeing that cute little face staring back at you for the first time. After having a list of 50 pictures written down, I decided to scrap that list and start over. This time, I put on my "agent" eyes and selected my top choices. Within a few hours of sending out the photos chosen for representation, I received emails requesting agent meetings for my little one. Stay tuned; that part is coming up. I can't wait to explain how that all happened!

STEP TWO

AN HONEST RESUME

"Be honest. Please don't exaggerate..."

The truth is that most children entering the acting business will not have extensive resumes. Even if you start them off super early, most of those credits might be commercials or print. It is still not customary to list every commercial or print job on an acting resume. The standard on a professional resume is to state, "Commercials: Conflicts Available Upon Request." Why? Because a casting director may see a Wells Fargo Bank commercial listed on your resume and not call you in for a Bank of America commercial, as this would be a conflict. The CD will have no idea that this commercial was shot two years ago or that there are currently no bank conflicts. They may not have time to check with you or your agent and wait for a response before sending audition notices.

RULES FOR RESUMES

So, what's the main reason to create a resume for a child actor just starting? You want to showcase their skills and potential. Before we get into the details, you need to know a few basic rules of resumes.

Rule #1: Be Honest

Please don't exaggerate, whether it's a leading role vs. background role or a beginner vs. advanced skill level. If your child has just started taking ballet lessons, don't claim they are a professional prima ballerina. Or, if they've just started taking Spanish classes, don't list Spanish as their second language. Your representatives and casting directors would prefer you tell the truth without embellishment. No one likes to feel misled. Hollywood is like one big, happy *Modern Family*. Just like your own family, people talk. And word gets around quickly. If people are going to talk, give them something positive to say.

Innocent and I went in for a commercial audition together (always lovely to audition with my baby), and the CD led us inside the room. I noted that she was friendly and seemed familiar with my son. However, I didn't remember us coming in to audition with her before. After we slated our names, she looked at the monitor, smiled, and said, "You want to hear a funny story?" From a casting director who could get you a job? Yes, please! "So, I was talking to a friend of mine, another casting director. I told her I was looking for a specific type of boy for this spot we're casting today. She said, 'have you heard of Innocent? He came in for one of my castings and is very good. You should call him in.' So, I saw your name in the submissions and figured there's got to be only one Innocent." It would be an understatement to say I left that audition, giving my son fist bumps and doing the electric slide. I was SO proud. I reminded him that there are eyes every-where, and every audition is an opportunity to make a great impression. Even if you don't get the part, you are building a reputation in this industry that will take you far and get you noticed. Welcome to the Family.

Rule #2: Don't be Desperate

Your child will mirror your example. It's ok, fantastic, and fabulous if your child doesn't have a list of 30 skills they can do at the child prodigy level. Sometimes your agents will call and inquire about your child's skill level in a particular area before submitting them for a project. If they have minimal skills in that area or none at all, be honest. Furthermore, don't approach the situation with the attitude of desperation. If a CD is casting a child who can speak fluent French by tomorrow at 2 pm, do not call a French coach for a 4-hour cram session today. How do I know this won't serve you or your child very well? Because, beloved, I am speaking from experience. At one point, I was *that* parent who felt I had to make every audition work— no matter what. This will only add to the stress and pressure you and your child feel. You may turn a once well-rounded, optimistic child into an anxiety-ridden human being with all sorts of "issues."

Before submitting Innocent for one audition, his agent called and asked if he could ride a scooter. I was honest and said it wasn't his forte, but Innocent had ridden a scooter (OK, good enough) ...once at a friend's house. I immediately went out to buy a scooter, and we practiced for a couple of hours before submitting the self-tape to show off his scooter-riding skills. Of course, Innocent was excited to get a new scooter since he had been asking for one for some time, but I was STRESSED! I wanted him to do well. The remainder of that day became all about riding the scooter. Whatever project or work I had scheduled for the day was put on hold because I thought it was my job as a good momager to ensure my child nailed that audition. In the end, he didn't get the job, and from then on, I told myself that I would never do that again.

Of course, right after that, I bought a chess set to teach my son chess one night because the part called for a child chess player. Don't mind me. All that matters is that I've learned my lesson. The right opportunity will come along for your child. Highlight your child's natural and legitimate skills, and don't force anything. Today, my baby is an outstanding scooter rider, by the way. But it came naturally with time and much practice. Parents, don't stress yourselves out, and don't sweat the small stuff.

WHAT GOES ON THE RESUME?

In addition to the signature headshot showing off their beautiful faces and unique personality, the resume is the icing on the cake, providing a well-rounded view of your sweetie pie. When your young actor is just starting, you must focus on their skills, hobbies, and personal strengths. One good thing to note is that a kid's resume allows much more flexibility and freedom than an adult resume. Once your child signs with an agent or manager, the new rep will guide you on the expected standards presentation. Until then, there are primary headings that you need to consider when putting together a resume for your child.

1. **Stats:** In the top left corner, put your child's name, hair color, eye color, weight, height, voice type (if they sing), and date of birth.

2. **Special Skills:** Include hobbies along with the various skills. Casting directors will pay close attention to this section because it will assist them in determining if your child is suitable for a specific role they may be casting. For example, if your child enjoys playing basketball

and is very good, this is your opportunity to highlight that skill. If there's a role for a young basketball player, your child will be one of the first in line to get that audition. If they can sing, dance, or play musical instruments, specify which styles and their level (i.e., beginning piano or intermediate piano). Other examples to include in this section would be sports, sport-like skills (juggling, jumping rope, hula-hoop, riding a bike, riding a scooter, skate-boarding), online content creation (YouTube channel), fishing, and modeling.

This section would also be the appropriate place to include that your child loves animals. Does this apply to one animal in particular? Be very specific if they fear any animal. These days, many kid shows have live animals on set. If dogs are on set and your child fears them, this may not be the right project for them. In Innocent's latest film, his agent asked if he liked dogs and his comfort level with them. Of course, my son loves dogs of all types, sizes, shapes, and colors! As of the writing of this book, we are currently on set with several dogs. (Their names are even listed on the call sheet!) If Innocent feared dogs and had panic attacks around them, this set would not be appropriate for him. You can also include industry-specific skills. For example, are they friendly, outgoing, a good listener, or a team player? Do they follow directions, read well, excel at memorization, get along with other kids and adults, or have an adventurous spirit? These basic skills are gold mines in child actors. Time is money—especially in this business. If a kid can't concentrate on set, and what should take an hour to film takes half a day, the producers won't be pleased when their budget goes over.

3. Community Involvement: When Innocent signed with his first manager, they wanted to know which charities he was involved in and what type of humanitarian efforts he enjoyed. Including such information shows your child's humane and empathetic side. Is your child in Boy Scouts or Girl Scouts? Do they volunteer to feed the homeless with your church or civic organization? Do they mentor other kids? Such activities speak to your child's character, which is essential to both directors and producers. Sometimes the biggest compliment I receive about Innocent is not necessarily how good of an actor he is (although he *is* good). It's how sweet he is on set, how he gets along well with other kids, and how he is respectful to the director and cast members. Your child's talent may get them in the door, but their character will maintain their position for years to come.

4. Education: If your little one is in school, you can list their academic and artistic achievements in this section. Did they receive any subject or class-specific awards (i.e., drama, spirit, math, science, spelling, or social studies)? Do they hold any offices in student government? This section would, of course, pertain to older kids new to the industry, but the goal is the same—showing their strengths and emphasizing what type of actor they might be on set. Suppose you have a kid who received the highest GPA in their fifth-grade class. This child will likely continue that spirit of excellence and commitment in their acting career. If your child attends acting school or has taken a commercial or on-camera class, list it here and include the teacher's name. It may not seem significant to you, but training is essential. As I said before, this industry is like a big family. Your agents, managers, casting directors, and directors may be familiar with many of these people. And people talk. This is a big plus if a prospective agent recognizes someone on your child's resume with an excellent reputation. It may take a simple call to someone listed on the resume to confirm that your budding actor has been a great student for the past two years and is nailing it in their On-Camera class. It could be the icing on the red velvet cake that prompts an agent to call your child in for a meeting.

5. Theater: When I first graduated college, most of my resume consisted of theater credits because I had not yet broken into the film or TV side of the business. This is fine. For your child who has no credits, you can list their theater productions at school or church. Just show that they are actively working on their craft. You can also include any dance or music performances in this section.

Once your child builds experience, some of these credits can be replaced as a more professional-based resume takes shape. I am amazed at my son's resume and how it has grown from when he first started! It's all a work in progress. Since age 3, Innocent has built a resume that could rival an adult actor's resume. It takes patience, diligence, and commitment. Don't be in a hurry to fill up the resume. Everything will come in due time.

Remember that a formatted resume is unnecessary for a young child just starting. When Innocent was three, he had nothing to put on a resume except his personality traits and special skills. When I first sent his cover letter to agents, I didn't include a resume. I had 7-8 pictures from his photo shoot, showing the best aspects of his personality. The cover letter was simple, requesting a meeting so that they could experience his fabulous personality for themselves. In hindsight, knowing what I know now, I would have probably done a little bit more to formulate some type of resume, no matter how small it might have been. What got Innocent in the door was the initial calling card— the headshot. His resume has been building for the past couple of years and is now one of the most vital parts of his portfolio that gets him the auditions.

STEP THREE

WORK PERMIT

Your Budding Actor Can't Work Without It
"Work permits are necessary and a part of the system under child labor laws to protect your precious one against exploitation and unsafe working conditions."

I remember the first time we received the starting paperwork from Innocent's agent after he was signed. Somehow, I didn't remember there being so many steps to starting a professional career in acting when I first landed in LA! But then again, I was a legal adult who could make my own decisions and didn't need all of the protections in place that your child actor will need. Work permit? *My 3-year-old requires a work permit; I* chuckled to myself. *Wow, am I ready for everything about to go down?* I hoped that, perhaps, he could land an agent, get an audition the first week, start working, and live happily ever after somewhere over the industry rainbow.

Work permits are simple to acquire, especially since you can do everything online. When I applied for Innocent's permit, I had to go into the Department of Labor sub-office and pick up a hard copy. Although the process has been improved, work permits can still be somewhat challenging, particularly at renewal time. I recommend that you begin the renewal process at least 60 days before the renewal date. You never know how long it will take. The wait times were particularly lengthy during the pandemic because there was a backlog and a rush to get work permits renewed once production resumed. I heard agents and managers relay stories of their clients not having updated work permits and losing significant jobs. Why? Because it's illegal for children to work in this industry without one. "But what if they have a permit, and it's just expired? Like a driver's license ... is there a grace period?" Nope. Services to expedite the renewal process are available but come with a fee.

THE BASICS

You may want to get your highlighters ready for this section. Highlight the areas specific to your child's age group. Let's get started!

A Work Permit is necessary for minors 15 days to 18 years old (*ARTICLE 6. Duties of Employer [49160 -*

49165], 1976). Before 15 days, a baby's only concerns should be sleeping, eating, eliminating, and getting lots of love. If you're anything like me, you will be shocked to know that a kid can start working at 15 days old! WOW! I thought beginning my son's career at three was ambitious. But it happens. Some parents may already be in a Hollywood family and want to bring the newest member on board as quickly as possible. (No judgment. It's all good!) These permits are required in states with a relatively large representation of TV and film productions—California, Georgia, New York, and Louisiana. The DLSE (Division of Labor Standards Enforcement) issues them through the Department of Industrial Relations. You can apply online (the most accessible way) or in person at your local Labor Commissioner's Office. Unlike applying for a passport, your child does not have to be present to apply if you bring all the requested documents.

A work permit is valid for six months. If you are applying online, the renewal portal opens within 60 days of the required renewal. I suggest getting an early start and clicking "Renew" as soon as possible. The process online is straightforward. If your child is school-aged, you will need an updated copy of the school affidavit supporting your child's request to work. If school is not in session, you must upload the latest school report showing your child in good standing. You must renew this permit every six months until your child is 18. After that, they're on their own!

In California, every minor working in the entertainment industry must obtain an "Entertainment Work Permit" from the DLSE. An application can be downloaded at **https://www.dir.ca.gov/dlse/Entertainment-Work-Permit.htm**. It can take up to 45 days (or longer) for the 6-month work permit to be issued after applying. Although an agent or manager will sign a minor without a work permit, obtaining this document will be among the top priorities, along with the Coogan account (Step 4), which goes hand in hand. The DLSE website details the necessary documents and requirements for each age group.

Necessary Documents

Ages 15 days - Kindergarten

You will need a certified birth certificate, baptismal certificate, or passport. This is required to prove the birth date of your child. Suppose you don't have any of these documents. In that case, you can also secure an official letter from the hospital where your child was born verifying the date of birth.

For children younger than one-month-old, you will also need a medical certification from a licensed physician who is board-certified in pediatrics to verify that your child is at least 15 days old. I know you may be eager to show off the cutest kid in the world, but your little buttercup can't legally work until they are 15 days old. The physician will also need to attest that your baby was full term, had average birth weight, and is physically healthy and capable of handling the stresses of filmmaking. The focus is to ensure that their lungs, heart, and immune systems are appropriately developed because this could be a liability for production.

School-Aged Children

For children in grades 1-12, the school will need to provide an authorized certification stating that your child is in good academic standing and attendance is satisfactory. This certification must contain the school's official seal or stamp; otherwise, it is considered invalid. Please note that there are times that the school district will NOT approve or send an affidavit. Applying for a work permit is not automatic. Your child must be in good standing.

A close friend of mine, who is also in the entertainment industry, wanted his kids in the business. Both children were of school age; one excelled in school, but the other did not. When he approached the principal for the school affidavit, he assumed it would be automatic and that his older child (with academic concerns) would simply be passed through. My friend and his wife were shocked and upset when their older son was not given the school's approval. Teachers expressed concerns because he was not achieving at grade level, and the additional stressor of working could cause further problems. With no other options, the rest of the family members continued to book jobs together without the older son. Luckily, after only one semester at a different school, his academic performance improved, and he could join his family in the audition and booking process. The entire family is now very successful and are all working actors.

Before I experienced this business firsthand, I wondered why colleges insisted that young athletes sit out a semester if their grades were not up to par. I used to think, *This is sports, and the team depends on them! Why should grades stop them from playing a sport which focuses on team building, support, and team success?* Once I started working with Innocent and watching the plight of other industry children, I began to understand. This industry, just like sports, is unpredictable. It's not a sure thing. You can have 50 auditions and only book one job or none! You can play 50 games and never get drafted to an NBA or professional team.

College-Aged Minors

When dealing with minors and college-aged kids, it is the responsibility of the adults, child labor laws, and college policymakers to ensure that the youth succeed academically first and foremost. Although it may not secure a million-dollar job, finishing that education and graduating is an essential requirement, especially for very young kids. Although there are teachers on set, they do not provide detailed instruction as they would in a traditional classroom. In our situation, for example, Innocent's teacher at school usually provides photocopies of classwork he would miss. On set, Innocent sits in a classroom with kids of various ages and is expected to do the worksheets alone, asking for assistance if needed. What if he were already behind in school and failing? In that case, I can see how this would completely disrupt the flow of his education. The other education option would be homeschooling. This brings us to our following scenario regarding work permits.

Home School

If your child is homeschooled and attends either an online, virtual, or private institution, the principal's office of the homeschool program will need to complete the school record form or provide a recently dated and signed letter on school letterhead indicating that your child is satisfactory in all their academic subjects, attendance, and health. The parent or guardian must complete the form if your child is not enrolled in an official homeschool program. You will need an affidavit from the local school district, county office of education, or state board of education in your area (*ARTICLE 5.5. Independent Study [51744 - 51749.6]*, 1976).

EXTENUATING CIRCUMSTANCES

Here's the good news! If your child is *that kid* who gets an agent, lands an audition, and books the role all within a week, never fear! There's a little caveat gem for you. You can apply for a 10-day temporary work permit for only $50! Woo hoo! The permit is available immediately after you send the payment online and is valid for ten days. Hopefully, your child can film within those ten days, and all will be well.

You don't need the SSN or the school affidavit for this temporary work permit. Your child must be between 15 days and 15 years old to receive this immediate approval. If your child is 15 days to 1 month old, you must submit a medical certification. You will receive an email confirmation within 24 hours, and you can download and print the work permit. Unfortunately, your 16 and 17-year-old actors are not eligible for this temporary permit. Once the temporary work permit is granted, you will still need to obtain a regular work permit, which will go through the normal process. There are no fees to apply for a standard work permit, and all renewals are free. Again, you should begin the renewal process at least 6-8 weeks before the permit expires.

If your child books another job after the 10-day temporary work permit has expired, there are independent services that may be able to assist (for a fee) in expediting your work permit. The production company may also send a letter to the Department of Labor in your area indicating that your permit needs to be expedited due to impending work. I have had to do this in Innocent's case. His permit took quite some time due to a backlog in the system, and his agent asked the production company to send a letter of employment offer. When I emailed the DOL, they asked that this letter be sent on official letterhead. Once this was done, Innocent's permit was ready for print and renewed within that week. Yes, all this preparation is much work, but things are in place to assist you along the way. No one wants your child to miss the job of a lifetime. I've learned that, for the most part, all entities work together to protect your child, first and foremost.

TRANSFERABILITY

Are work permits nationally or globally recognized? No, they are not. You will need to apply for a work permit in every state (or country) that requires your child to have one to work. Generally, production will assist you in getting these work permits if the child is hired in one state but must travel to another state to work. If the minor is Los Angeles based and is booked on a film in Atlanta, they will also need to apply for a work permit in Georgia. When Innocent booked a movie in Vancouver, his California work permit was still valid. However, he needed to be approved for a work permit in Vancouver. We also had to ensure his passport was up to date. The Canadian consulate requested proof that his passport would not expire before the work permit expired. Although this was the case, production had their team of lawyers intercede with customs to approve the permit, pending passport renewal. Again, the system is put in place to protect children, and everything works for their good. These systems can work together to help us overcome any loopholes we may encounter.

COST

This whole business of work permits is not a money-making scheme. Applying and renewing (unless you need the 10-day temporary permit) is free. **Work permits are necessary and a part of the system under child labor laws to protect your precious one against exploitation and unsafe working conditions.** Everything is working in tandem. Having the school approval ensures that your child maintains good academic standing and doesn't fail out of school to go to work.

"Back in the day," parents could take children out of school to work on farms and do other jobs because they needed to help support the family. These days, it's illegal because it's not in the child's best interest. Reps may periodically remind their clients to ensure work permits are up to date. However, it is ultimately the parent or guardian's responsibility to ensure everything is copacetic. Make sure you keep track because you don't want to be *that* parent always "cutting it close" in terms of not knowing if your child will be available to work due to an expired permit. In these days of fast turnaround and bookings, the last thing you want to happen is for your child to book a job that starts the next day, but their work permit expires next week, and you forgot to renew. You don't want your agent or manager and your child to decline a life-changing opportunity because they are out of compliance. Even though your adorable child is perfect for a role, it is illegal for a production company to hire a child without a valid (non-expired) work permit.

STEP FOUR

COOGAN ACCOUNT

Money Talks: Coogan account and Protecting Your Child's Future

"The sacrifice a parent or guardian will make is far bigger than the monetary gains you may experience, especially in the beginning."

C an you imagine turning 18 and having a substantial trust fund waiting for you? You would be part of that elite group of people we see on TV who seem to have a leg up in life because their wealthy parents or grandparents left them a big inheritance. This is essentially what a Coogan account is. The only difference is that your child is *working* to build their trust fund. SAGAFTRA.org describes a Coogan account as a "blocked account" or "trust account." Per SAG, these are required by the state of

California, New York, Louisiana, and New Mexico (*CHAPTER 3. Contracts in Art, Entertainment, and Professional Sports [6750 - 6753], 1992*).

In most cases, you must prove that you have one of these trust accounts for your minor before getting a work permit. Per SAG-AFTRA, in the United States, 15% of the gross amount of your child's earnings for each job must be remitted to this account within 15 days of employment (*CHAPTER 3. Contracts in Art, Entertainment, and Professional Sports [6750 - 6753], 1992*). When your child books a job, you must submit proof of this account to the production company. The production company will deposit these funds immediately after a check is issued.

It was a little confusing when I first applied for Innocent's Coogan account. I wasn't entirely sure what the account was, and I found that some bank reps did not know what I was talking about. One conversation went something like this:

Me: "Hi, my son just signed with an agent, and he's an actor. I need to open a Coogan account for him."

Banker: "A Coogan account? Do you mean a savings account?"

Me: "No, a Coogan account … you know, the one that kid actors can't touch until they're 18."

Banker: "Well, you can open a savings account for him and keep it until he's 18."

Me: "No, I need a Coogan account. The one a parent can't access even if I wanted to."

Banker: "Hmm, Ok ... I've never heard of that."

I was shocked. How could a banker in Los Angeles, with all the most famous child actors, not know what I'm talking about?? I hit the pavement and visited a few banks before I found a specific Wells Fargo Bank branch that understood my request. All the while, I wondered why we needed an account with a proverbial parent-proof lock until Innocent turns 18.

HISTORY

Once I learned about the history of the Coogan account, its necessity and reasoning became very clear. You may wonder, as I did, *wouldn't all parents want the best for their children and guard that 15% with the utmost care without touching it until they are 18?* Ideally, yes. However, many children need that security put in place legally. This security is even more intense than those government bonds our grandmothers used to purchase for us every birthday and holiday. While they were challenging to cash out, a Coogan account makes withdrawals nearly impossible until your child's 18th birthday, unless you get an emergency court order.

Does anyone remember Uncle Fester from *The Adams Family*? You know, the round one with the bald head, sunken eyes, and permanent mischievous grin? Well, he started as a child actor and was highly successful. When I say highly successful, I mean he amassed millions of dollars as a child actor in the early 1900s! Charlie Chaplin discovered him in 1919 at the tender age of seven. He landed the role of the funny man's sidekick in the box office hit, *The Kid*. That movie was his breakout role and earned him a title as one of the first child stars in the history of Hollywood. His name was John Leslie ("Jackie") Coogan (SAGAFTRA.org).

In 1935, when Jackie was 20 years old, his father was killed in a car accident. Up until that point, his father had been doing a decent job managing Jackie's resources. By the time Jackie turned 21, he had decided it was time to cash out and have access to the money he'd earned. His mother and stepfather refused his request. Unfortunately, it was speculated and proven that they had spent his 3–4-million-dollar earnings extravagantly without his knowledge. That sum is the equivalent of 44-59 million dollars today! Let me repeat … 44-59 MILLION dollars. Wow! Devastated, Jackie filed a formal lawsuit against his mother and former manager for his earnings in 1938 (*Jackie Coogan*, 2022).

During that time, a child's income belonged to the parents, who had the authority to dispense with it as they pleased. In 1939, the "California Child Actor's Bill" (also known as the "Coogan law") was enacted to protect the earnings of these child actors who would soon become adults and need their money (Terry, 2018). Although he never fully recouped his fortune, Jackie recovered a tiny portion ($126,000 of the $250,000 that remained (*Jackie Coogan*, 2022). He continued to work in the entertainment industry and eventually landed the role of Uncle Fester in *The Addams Family*. What happened to Jackie was outrageous. He was left with hardly any money from his childhood fortune. He had to ask for help from his former co-stars, even Charlie Chaplin, before he could continue his career and transition to an adult actor (Robinson, 1985). I can't imagine what he must have felt. His life might have been vastly different if this law had existed during that time. Working as an actor for enjoyment vs. working because you need money to eat and make ends meet (after making millions of dollars) is unfathomable. After hearing this story and others like it, I completely understand why a special account is necessary. Jackie Coogan paved the way to ensure that child actors would have financial security after spending their entire childhood entertaining the world.

IN MODERN TIMES

I did not know the proper name for the type of account I was seeking when we started. As I mentioned, some banks are unfamiliar with the Coogan account because that name is industry specific. The proper terminology is *Block Trust Account*, so make sure to use this term when you go into the bank to inquire. The term *blocked* refers to the 15% from each paycheck withheld, reserved, and *blocked* from anyone's use until your child turns 18. On their website, SAG-AFTRA provides a partial list of banks offering Coogan accounts: SAG-AFTRA Federal Credit Union, Actors Federal Credit Union, Bank of the West, City National Bank, First Entertainment Credit Union, Morgan Stanley/Smith Barney, Union Bank of California, and Wells Fargo. The rules for opening this type of account may vary from bank to bank. Wells Fargo, for example, requires the minor to either be employed or hold an employment offer. Once the account is set up, they will issue a letter of proof that the account is active. The parent or guardian setting up the account is listed as the trustee or beneficiary. Production will ask you for the document when they send the paperwork you must complete each time your child begins work on a new project. In addition to proof of the account, other paperwork in this packet would include the contract (deal memo), tax information, safety information, etc. The list of paperwork is detailed and generally emailed to you or provided once you arrive on set. Once production has the account and routing number, they can deposit 15% of the wages directly into the trust account.

At the beginning of 2001, SAGAFTRA.org confirmed the Coogan law made it official that minors' earnings in the entertainment industry are their property, not the property of their parents. Since children are too young to control their money legally, the parent or guardian must oversee their finances until adulthood. California Law specifically governs the earnings of the minor. It establishes that 15% of earnings must immediately be held in the blocked account. It also shows a *fiduciary* relationship between the parent or guardian and the working child (*CHAPTER 3. Contracts in Art, Entertainment, and Professional Sports [6750 - 6753]*, 1992). Fiduciary as an adjective means "involving trust, especially concerning the relationship between a trustee and a beneficiary." As a noun, it means "trustee." The relationship establishes trust that the parent or guardian will do what is suitable for the child in managing their earnings properly. After opening the Coogan account, the bank provides the documents that list the parent as the trustee. A one-sheet document lists the bank's name, account number, and address. Production will ask for this information as soon as employment is offered, so please keep this handy on your smartphone, computer, or as a hard copy.

Nationally

As mentioned previously, blocked trust accounts are mandatory in the following states: California, New

York, Illinois, Louisiana, and New Mexico. Although they function in basically the same manner, the names may be different. California calls them Coogan accounts. In New York, the accounts are called UTMA (Uniform Transfers to Minors Act) or UGMA (Uniform Gifts to Minors Act). They can be opened in any bank that meets the requirements of UGMA and UTMA. In Illinois and New Mexico, the accounts are called blocked trust accounts and can be opened in all banks. However, in some states, these accounts are only mandated if the minor earns more than $1000.00 for each job.

As a parent, I feel extreme satisfaction and accomplishment whenever I see my son's Coogan account growing. After Innocent has finished a job, I get an alert from Wells Fargo showing the 15% deposited. The deposited money is like a gift that Innocent gets to unwrap when he's an adult. Isn't that wonderful?

Internationally

Although the United States law indicates that 15% of wages must go into a blocked account, other countries may have different rates. While filming *Ivy + Bean* in Vancouver, 25% of Innocent's salaries had to be deposited. This is the standard rule for ACTRA (The Alliance of Canadian Cinema, Television, and Radio Artists). Since a Canadian company ran the production, Innocent fell under this rule, and 25% was deposited into his trust account. Although I was initially under the impression that it would be the standard 15% per SAG-AFTRA rules, I was very OK with 25% going in. I saw it as an opportunity for him to bank even more significant savings in a shorter period. Some parents are uncomfortable with even the 15% being held out, but each situation is different.

A TRUTH

Since we are on the subject of money, I feel this is an excellent time to tell you the truth about child acting and money. The idea of having a child actor as a "get rich quick scheme" is a misconception. Some people will make insensitive comments, i.e., "Your son is in the movies, you're rich now," or "I'm sure you're enjoying all that money your son is making." Oh, and be ready for "Uh, since you all are making money now, can I borrow some?" Showbiz Parents who are reading this understand the journey. It can be upsetting and frustrating because people just don't get it. No. Having a child actor is NOT a way to make fast money. Being in the industry is a respectable way to assist your child in achieving their dreams and goals. At the same time, you're helping them build a trust account that will be useful when they are adults.

Contrary to popular belief, many parents still WORK their jobs or careers. Why? Because they need to keep a roof over their child's head, food on the table, and clothes on their back—just like any other parent. At times, one parent may have to sacrifice their career to become the professional assistant, set parent, driver, coach, and tutor to their talented bundle of joy. There is a trend of parents with working child actors who work to maintain their careers even when they are away on location or on set. The move toward telecommuting jobs has been beneficial for these parents.

AN EXAMPLE

A dear friend of mine is the primary breadwinner of her family, and she has four children. Her son, Jack, is a working child actor and has landed leading roles in many projects. My friend (let's call her Jane) can be found on set with her computer open, working on her telecommute job between takes and even while her son is shooting on set! She received so much attention from the directors, producers, and other moms on set, who marveled at her dedication. The producers eventually provided her with a workspace during the day because her son, due to his age, could work at least nine hours per day. Jane could not afford to give up those hours every working day to sit on set, hang out, and talk with the other parents. As I said, she is the primary breadwinner for her four kids, so her show must go on. The acting business is not secure. Most people understand that on some level. You may get a job today and not have another for the next couple of months or longer. Unless there's an alternate source of income to maintain household expenses, it's not wise for a parent to quit their job after their child's first booking. Let me illustrate what I mean, and then I'm sure you will understand.

Jack books a supporting role in a major film, and his contract is for $50,000. Once word gets out on the street, distant relatives start calling Jane with one request after another. Their children need school clothes, help to pay rent, or they lose their job; the list goes on. They assume Jane is now "in the money" because her son has booked a huge film, and why shouldn't she help every single one of her family members? Jane's son has a manager, an agent, and an entertainment lawyer to negotiate contracts. Every team member gets their money "off the top" before taxes. The manager has been contracted for 15%, so their take will be $7,500. Jack is now at $42,500. The agent is contracted for 10%, which is $5,000, and now Jack is at $37,500. The agent suggested that Jack hire an entertainment lawyer to ensure everything was correct in the contract. The lawyer's compensation is 5% to negotiate the deal, so they will take $2,500. Jack is now at $35,000. Jack is working in Los Angeles, and production will "block" 15% to put directly in the Coogan account. Jack now banks an additional $7,500 in his Coogan account and is down to $27,500. Oh, Uncle Sam will need his portion as well. Although Jack is a minor and can be claimed by his parents, he is still taxed as "Single" in the highest tax bracket, which averages 30% for all federal, state, SDI, etc., taxes.

Uncle Sam will collect $15,000, and Jack's take home may be $12,500. From $50,000 to $12,500. If you don't believe me, DM me, and I'll show you some of Innocent's paychecks. (Just kidding, I won't. You'll have to trust me).

When I say "take-home," this is the standard term in the industry for a child's upkeep. The remaining portion is paid to the parent or guardian to assist with bills associated with the child. This can include transportation, headshots, passport fees, resume services, sports classes, private school fees, voice, music, acting lessons, union dues, audition wardrobe, etc. This can be anything to help maintain and further your child's career. Do you see why my friend Jane needs to continue working? You can understand a parent's frustration when people comment about enjoying their kids' money and getting rich or asking why the parent is still working their regular job.

This part may deter some, but that's ok. It needs to. If your child is from the USA and books a job in Canada for a Canadian production company, the standard 15% going into Coogan would be 25% off the top, with an additional flat tax rate of 25%. Adjusting for those numbers, Jane is working with $10,000 for child upkeep. Beloved, these numbers are real. **The sacrifice that a parent or guardian will make is far more significant than the monetary gains you may experience, especially in the beginning.** But it shouldn't be about the money. It can't be. The driving force

MUST be assisting your young performer in achieving their destiny. So, the next time you get those ugly comments, please feel free to bookmark this page as a quick reference and tell them, "Read this, please, and thank you." You're welcome.

STEP FIVE

REPPED: MANAGERS AND AGENTS

"Get in with a great agency as a kid, do well, and you can transition to your adult career with a team that has been invested in your career from an early age."

Landing an agent or manager is a unique process that must be taken seriously. Once an actor is signed to representation, they are considered "repped" or "represented." Even adult actors find it challenging to land representation, so beginning at a young age is a head start. Once your little one is at this stage of the game, congratulations are in order! The fun has just begun.

When I first came to Los Angeles, getting representation was about *who you know*. At that time, we had to send hard copy photos to each prospective agent and pray for an interview. Or, if you were lucky, you could be referred by someone who knew someone who might bring you in for that interview and sign you. In the internet age, the submission process is much cheaper and faster. With the click of a button, you can submit to dozens of agents without spending the postage or money on photo reproductions. Although it is still recommended to have hard-copy photos, I don't recall the last time I needed to use any. Even now, Innocent's printed headshots are framed and used as photographs around the house because we don't need them anymore. I would have never imagined that! And yes, all his current representatives were secured without using printed photos. Everything was via electronic measures. And now, the million-dollar question: What is the difference between an agent and a manager, and are they both necessary? I am so glad you asked because I'm about to dish the honey milk tea and shortbread cookies on this topic!

AGENTS

An agent is the principal steward of an actor's career path and should assist in branding, networking, public relations, and career development. The role of an agent is to arrange meetings and auditions with casting directors, agents, and producers. The process begins with submitting their clients for roles on Breakdown Express daily. This site lists available parts in various projects. Agents are also permitted to negotiate your child's work contracts. In California, every agent must be licensed by the State where their business is located, and that license must be renewed yearly. They must also undergo a background check, fingerprinting, and registration as a corporation or LLC. This protects the clients and ensures that your representative is legit, which is especially important when someone will be handling your child's money.

Agents are generally paid a commission of 10% of their client's gross salary. When your child signs with an agency, you typically sign a check authorization giving your agent authorization to collect and cash the checks. The agent will put the money in their account, take their commissions, and send the remainder your way. Therefore, most of your child's payments will be written from the agent's account. The agent should also provide you with a copy of the official statement before rep commissions have been taken out.

According to the California Department of Industrial Relations Division of Labor Standards Licensing and Registration Unit, the talent agent must put up a bond worth $50,000 to ensure payment to their clients. An agent's roster generally consists of dozens of actors of all types and ages. Agents tend to have more actors on their rosters than managers, submitting for dozens or hundreds of actors daily. Within an agency, there may be different departments. For example, *Agency A* may have the following departments: Youth, Young Adults, Adults, Voice-Overs, Commercials, Print, Literary, etc. Different agents will be assigned to each department with their respective client rosters. However, all clients will be listed under the same agency.

Our Experience

After months of hitting the pavement in Los Angeles when I first arrived, I spent many hours putting head-shots, resumes, and cover letters in those brown 8 x10 envelopes (I bought them in bulk), hoping and praying to get a call for a meeting. And yes, I was referred to my initial manager by a previous director who had cast me in their low-budget film. The appointment was given to me as a favor. Thankfully, our journey in finding an agent for Innocent was surprisingly straightforward. I had no clue that my three-year-old would be signed with an agent within three days! It was unheard of in my experience.

The Process

After perfecting this process by coaching parents and their talented children, I have decided that our formula works. There's no guarantee that everything will work for every person, but I can tell you that this has been the best process for our Showbiz Kids team.

1. Find a Photographer

After Innocent's first headshot session, I chose the top 3-6 photos to represent both commercial and theatrical looks. The eventual goal was for him to be signed in all areas (also known as "across the board").

Most of his photos then were commercial because I knew that landing a commercial agent would lead to print and eventually theatrical and voice-over. I was so happy with his pictures, and every time I looked at that cute little face, I knew it would only be a matter of time before he found great success in this field.

Innocent's photographer, Angel Bousquet, captured his beautiful, fun-loving, and even comedic personality within those photos. Everything he did to engage Innocent successfully translated into the images. I was there for the entire session and was pleased to see the finished product. For a moment, I ceased being a momager and was just a proud mama saying, "Look at my Baby!!!"

Since then, Innocent has shot with 1 or 2 other photographers. But for the first four years, we consistently sought out Angel. Why? Because my son worked well with Angel, and it's always great to maintain consistency and comfort with young children. It's also good to get input from other photographers when you feel it is time. Most recently, we did a headshot session with Matt Stasi to gather more theatrical looks, which turned out amazing! The photo you see on the cover is from that session; that says it all! The one problem we've had with all of our photographers is that we have too many good headshots from which to choose! When that is the case with your photographer, you know you've got some keepers!

2. Do Your Research

I was very well versed in the world of adult actors. I wasn't as familiar with the child actor's world. Where do we turn when someone has a question and needs a quick answer? GOOGLE, of course! It was vital for me to find someone who represents children because, as I've discovered, this population is quite distinct and has its own sets of special needs. I searched "top 10 agents for kids," which gave me a list of results. (The lists will change yearly, so the results today would likely not be the same names I found.) I researched each of their websites and found their preferred method of communication. Some asked to be sent an email, while others asked for submissions directly on their website.

3. Introductory Email

After I had my list, I crafted a cover letter to include in the body of an email and attached the headshots therein. This is what my email included:

Subject Line: Innocent Ekakitie (3) Seeking Representation Across the Board.
Body: Hi (Agent Name), please see attached photos of Innocent Ekakitie. He's seeking representation in all areas and would be honored to have a meeting with you to show off his fabulous personality! ;-)

I included my son's full name, date of birth, height, clothing size, shoe size, weight, eye color, and hair color. Then, I listed myself as his contact, along with my phone number. I wanted to give them the basic information they would see on a resume to determine if they needed his type on their roster or not.

I also added commercial and theatrical shots within the body of the email. Since then, I have further refined my process by working with other children and their parents. The best way to submit the photos is via links (i.e., WeTransfer or Dropbox) which someone can open with or without a pre-existing account. Including photos directly within an email can take time to download.

On March 10th at 3:01 pm, I sent *Agent A* the introductory email. I received a response that same day at 3:37 pm stating, "We would love to meet him. Can you bring him in this Monday at 11:25 am?" I responded, "Hmm, let me check my schedule to see if we're free." Just kidding! I replied, "Absolutely! Thank you so much, *Agent A*. We really appreciate the opportunity to meet with you. We'll see you at 11:25 am Monday."

Remember to keep it simple. Our email was just a few sentences, but that's all that is necessary. You don't have to sell young children yet. That's one of the benefits of breaking into the industry at such a young age. As I've shared, I had been acting since I was a child but didn't get to New York until college and Los Angeles until graduate school. Getting my agent was not as simple as it was for Innocent because a "burden of proof" rests with an adult actor. You've got to sell yourself and let your prospective rep know why they should call you for a meeting. And it would help if you did this without sounding green or desperate. Representatives understand that many kids at age three won't have a long list of training, classes, and roles under their belts. **Get in with a great agency as a kid, do well, and you can transition to your adult career with a team that has been invested in your career from an early age.**

4. Agent Interview

Innocent was charming and very much himself. I knew I could coach him, but his personality would ultimately get him signed. I told him to shake the agent's hand and tell them, "It was nice meeting you." After the meeting, he extended his hand to the agent and said, "My Mom says I should shake your hand." Of course, the agent thought that was cute, and we all shared a sweet laugh. The takeaway is to let your kids be themselves! If they are destined to be in this industry, they will make the best impressions naturally. We signed with that agency the same day; the rest is history.

MANAGERS

Agents and Managers act as strategic partners to help build a successful career. Both work on commissions. Although they work in tandem, there are some differences between the two, which differentiate how they can operate on your behalf.

Credential Differences

The Screen Actors Guild

Managers are neither regulated nor franchised by SAG-AFTRA. They can, however, be affiliated with SAG, which indicates they are in good standing with the union, and the union recognizes them as a legitimate talent manager.

State Level

The state does not require managers to be licensed. For that reason, they cannot negotiate your employment offers. However, they can provide their input to the team. The official negotiation is left up to the agent. A manager can submit you for an audition and give you the information regarding callbacks, etc. However, when it comes time to negotiate contracts, managers cannot negotiate. If you don't have an agent, the Talent must do the negotiations but can take advice from the Manager.

Since a manager does not have to be licensed by the state, whom you select as a talent manager could be anyone—even Great Aunt Myrtle or Mom. You might be their only client and receive the most incredible personal attention in this case. Before I had my son, I was friends with a popager who had done very well with his child actor (now transitioned into an adult actor). He worked hard for his son and worked closely with his son's agent. He eventually set up a company and officially became his son's manager. This was a huge step. It is an intense job when you, as a parent or family member, decide to set up your own management company to represent your loved one. We signed with a manager when Innocent was five because I realized I needed to turn it over to the professionals if I wanted to build a solid team with industry connections. I knew I couldn't be a manager 100% of the time while maintaining my career. I needed to be his momager, which meant that while I did the groundwork, I still kept my position as Mommy.

Clientele

A manager typically has a smaller client roster than an agent. They can provide personalized career guidance and advice from headshots to hiring business managers or lawyers. This direct interaction can be priceless, as an agent may not have the time to speak to you directly about specific career moves. For example, Innocent had been with his agent for about two years, and we were happy with everything. However, he was still being submitted for commercials and print, and we were ready for him to move to the next level theatrically. I implemented the same process in seeking theatrical representation, and just like clockwork, we received responses and meeting offers. One famous agent in Beverly Hills wanted to sign Innocent "across the board" (the one I mentioned in the introduction). We were torn because we liked our current commercial agent, but we were ready to take a more theatrical direction.

His manager, who was still new to us then, suggested we consider the move wisely. The agent who wanted to sign him was more well-known for their extensive commercial and print campaigns. "Innocent can book commercials and print all day," she said. "But if you want him to transition into a serious actor, it's best to go with an agency with a strong theatrical department." She also pointed out that it would be better to remain with our existing agency because we had been with them since he was three. They were already highly invested in his success.

She called the owner of the current agency and requested an audition for their Theatrical division. Shortly after, they agreed to a theatrical meeting with Innocent. We spent a week working on a magnificent monologue. After the meeting, they decided to sign Innocent in the theatrical division! Within two weeks, he booked his first major television show, starring in Apple TV's *Little America*. We would not have been able to get that one-on-one attention with an agent at the time. He was too new in the game. This decision positively affected Innocent's career, and we are still experiencing the afterglow effects of Kat Gordon's excellent advice and management!

Payment

A manager usually takes 10-15% of gross income on all projects, whether or not they procure the audition. It's crucial to understand that in developing a successful and long-term career for your child, there is no time for the mentality of, "You didn't get the audition, so why should we pay you?" Ultimately, everyone works as a team. Everyone is in the trenches submitting, making calls, and advising. So, when the time comes, everyone benefits from the success of the work they have put in. Agents and managers do not make money until your child books. Even if it takes one year of working for their client, they must have the patience to know that they've made a good decision in bringing you onto their roster. Once your child becomes a series regular on a show, the pay is much higher per episode. It's neither fair nor legal to say, "His agent got the audition, so we shouldn't have to pay the manager," or vice versa. Teamwork makes the Dream Work. And the ultimate goal is to help your child's dreams become a reality.

Our Experience

When Innocent was five, he had been with a commercial agent for two years. My friend's son was signed with a manager and told me how great it was to get that one-on-one advice and help. They felt the agent didn't give them the attention they needed to help guide their son's young career. My friend called the manager and told her that she needed to meet with a fabulous little actor named Innocent. I sent her his updated resume (which was growing by this time), a few headshots, and a cover letter. Even with the referral, I went through the official introductory process as I had done before. We set up an appointment via Zoom, and the manager was able to speak with us. She fell in love with Innocent and his personality and asked to sign with us that day.

As I mentioned, Kat was crucial in helping us decide to remain with his current agent and setting up an appointment for theatrical representation within the agency. Although she secured the initial audition for the lead role of "Brian" on *Little America*, the agency negotiated the contract. We were on our way to New York/New Jersey for three weeks of filming. We received first-class treatment! A fancy car service transported us from our front door to the airport. We flew first class, and when we arrived in New York, a driver met us at the gate, holding up a sign with our last name. All the hotel bookings and accommodations were taken care of. We stayed in a hotel worth hundreds of dollars per night, were paid per diem, and had a driver to shuttle us back and forth for every rehearsal, fitting, and filming. Kat and our agent worked together to ensure everything ran smoothly. I marked this pivotal point as the start of Innocent's career as a serious, professional actor.

REMEMBER

Parents, there will be sacrifices on all sides. You know what that means if you are also in the entertainment industry. You can get a booking today and have to pack up and be ready to go tomorrow. When Innocent booked *Little America*, I had already been booked to sing for a state-side memorial service in Africa. My ticket was purchased, and my hotel was booked. When I got the call from Kat, I scrambled for a while to decide what to do. Innocent's Dad is also in the industry, and he couldn't cancel the gigs for which he was booked for those weeks. When I told Kat my predicament, she even offered to travel with Innocent for those weeks, but I knew my 5-year-old would need his Mommy with him.

After a few tears, I decided that I would have to be the one to sacrifice. I called the person who had booked me for the singing job. Surprisingly, her response was, "Of course, you have to go with Innocent! This is a chance of a lifetime and will help his career! We completely understand."

I appreciated Kat's understanding of my dilemma. She was sympathetic as I processed everything and expressed my feelings about having to sacrifice an important event. I was honest about feeling "some type of way" concerning production not being flexible about us changing guardians for that week. Dad would be able to come in the first week, and I could come in the last weeks after my gig, but that would not be possible. It would have to be one parent or guardian throughout the duration. After I dried all my tears, I completely understood the reasoning behind that.

Building a team of invested people who know you and ultimately begin to feel like family is paramount. Everyone has their part to play in growing your child's career. Your agent and manager must get along well and respect each other's job. Transparency is also crucial. Innocent never received an audition from the agent without the manager being copied or vice versa. When he got his SAG card, the management company sent him a lovely gift full of treats, and my little one was THRILLED! He felt so special. An agent with hundreds of clients may not be able to notice such detail, but they will see when production needs to raise the price of per diem or when your checks are late. Like a family, everyone has unique qualities, characteristics, and strengths to make this life special, cohesive, and ultimately successful.

STEP SIX

ONLINE CASTING SITES: THE 3 "MUST HAVES"

"You should never sit back and allow anyone to control your child's destiny in this acting business. Be proactive, know what's out there, and do your part to make it happen!"

Although having a fantastic team is a must for all successful actors, the actor must do other things to further their success. A few online tools or casting sites are essential for every serious actor. You will need to set up your child's account, upload their photos, resume, and other pertinent information to each site, and update the information periodically. Neither an agent nor a manager can do this for you. It is up to the parent or guardian to ensure this is accomplished. Your child's representative won't be able to submit them for any projects until this step is completed. As we've established, the real work begins once your child is repped. Some may think that after securing representation, they can sit back and wait for the auditions and awesome jobs to roll in. Mmmm, not quite. Your job never ends until your child decides they can handle their career independently (along with their reps) as an adult actor. Like anything else, becoming a successful child actor is always a WIP (work in progress).

The process I'm about to detail can be completed *before* your child is signed to representation (most parents do this). During a pilot Innocent was shooting, I had the opportunity to speak with a few parents whose kids had not yet signed with an agent or manager. The kids expressed their desire to be in the industry. Hence, the parents took it upon themselves to begin the process and submit their children for various projects. One mom on set explained that she had seen the casting notice on one of the online casting sites, submitted her son, and her son was booked. As actors seek agents, these online sites have become very popular with independent actors. Unrepresented actors, however, may not have full access to every project listed on the official "breakdowns" as the agents and managers do.

Representation lends credibility to your child, and casting directors are likelier to cast the more prominent roles via agent or manager submissions. Setting up a profile with all three casting sites will save you time when your child is signed to representation. If the process goes quickly, as it did for Innocent, there is no need to worry. Information regarding the online casting sites should be included in their "new client" paperwork. You will be able to use the information in this chapter as a reference to gain a deeper understanding of these sites, how they are necessary for your child's career, and the differences among them.

ACTORS ACCESS

Actors Access (www.ActorsAccess.com) lists projects that are typically theatrical—TV and film roles. This site updates daily as new projects come out. It is a membership account and allows actors and their representatives to submit directly to the casting breakdowns. They release over 43,000 projects annually and have a database of over 1.1 million actors.

You can set up a free account for your child and upload two photos for free. Eventually, you will want to pay the additional price to add more photos. I like to keep a good variety of photographs uploaded to the site because each image can convey a different character and feeling. Giving your representatives plenty to work with to secure auditions is essential. Actors Access allows you to submit your child for a $2 per submission fee if you are unrepresented. Be aware that this can add up quickly because you may see quite a few projects on any given day that fit your child's specs. You will also pay to upload any video reels your child has. These reels may be clips from short films, commercials, or other jobs your child has booked and can give casting directors an idea of how your child looks on screen.

Clips should showcase your child's talents (i.e., singing, dancing, playing a musical instrument). If you already have an agent or manager, you shouldn't need to submit your child at this point. Their representative will handle the submissions moving forward. This doesn't mean you can't stay current with what's available. Suppose you have a good rapport with your manager, for example. In that case, you may send a quick email asking them to submit your child for a particular project, but you don't want to get into the habit of doing that. You should develop confidence in your child's representative and know they are doing their job and submitting your little actor for all appropriate projects.

I have a very close relationship with my manager, and there are times that I'll see projects through my online sites and inquire if he has submitted me. If he didn't, it might be because he felt I did not fit that particular role. For example, I may see a part that calls for an actor in a specific age range. Because I look younger, my manager may say, "You won't fit that because you look so much younger than the breakdown description." If I feel passionate about an opportunity and bring it to his attention, he is happy to submit me. Sometimes I'm right, casting will call me in, and I'll have an incredible audition and booking. Other times, I don't get the call, and we move on to the next one. The goal is to work closely with your representatives. It should become a dialogue regarding the course of your career instead of the actor leaving everything up to chance.

If your child is not yet represented, you can pay for an "Actors Access Plus Account" for $68 per year. This will allow unlimited submissions, eliminating the $2 per submission policy. With this subscription payment, you will also receive unlimited ECO cast auditions (we will discuss this later) and other perks. This is much more cost-effective and a better option until your child is signed.

Showfax Account

Signing up for the Actors Access PLUS account will get you access to Showfax. This site allows you to download the sides needed for an audition. For those unfamiliar with sides, these are partial scripts containing the dialogue your child will need to know for the audition. For example, suppose you are called to audition for a role on a TV show. In that case, casting will provide a "sides code." This is a security code you type in to view and download the necessary sides. If you are not given the code, you can quickly search and type in the project, casting director, or role. You will then be asked to log in with your Actors Access account. If you are a member of Plus, you can download unlimited sides for up to 24 projects per day. That is a lot because most actors may only use this feature a few times per week. You will have to pay a nominal fee for the sides if you are not a Plus member. Represented actors are generally sent the sides free of charge via their representatives, which are attached to the audition request.

CASTING NETWORKS—COMMERCIALS

You can access the sites to view commercial projects via www.CastingNetworks.com. Casting Networks, formerly LA Casting, has been the industry standard for agents and managers to send commercial break downs. Actors are also able to upload their information to submit for specific commercial roles themselves. Not every commercial breakdown will be available on this site, as with Actors Access. Some breakdowns are sent directly to representatives without being published. Having a profile on this site is a great way to get yourself in the door and seen by casting directors who may be looking for talent they haven't seen. Once you are represented, you will need to make a separate profile for each of your reps and your personal profile. Until recently, the actor had to input the entire profile from scratch, including uploading each photo. You can now copy a profile, which will automatically file under the new agent or manager profile. Whew! This has made our lives easier. Thank you, Casting Networks! Big shout out to you for streamlining and making the actor's life less complicated.

CASTING FRONTIER

Casting Frontier (www.CastingFrontier.com) is for actors, casting directors, and reps. Once you land representation, your agent will request that you sign up. Casting Frontier is primarily a commercial site but combines a bit of everything. You can submit for SAG-AFTRA, non-union, student films, music videos, voice-over, etc. It's a lovely site, and we quite enjoy it. You can sign up for an account with a basic plan for free. Other premium plans range from $75 to $95.99 per year. You'll be able to upload additional headshots and other multimedia files with unlimited project submissions.

Although Innocent's agents and manager submit him for everything, I'm still able to receive daily alerts from these casting sites, so I'm aware of the projects that are out there. A bonus of these sites is that they will send an email alert when your child matches a particular role, using the statistics filter you add to your profile. For example:

- Casting Networks will send an email stating, "New Role Fit for You! Hi, Innocent. We've found a new role from (Casting Company) that matches your profile criteria. Submit to this role today and get one step closer to booking your next job."
- Actors Access will hit us up and say, "Projects match your profile, Innocent. Our exclusive "Advanced Roles Notification" feature at Actors Access has just posted the following role in the following project that fits your profile. Click the links to view each project, and you can submit immediately if interested …"
- Casting Frontier keeps us in the loop by notifying us, "New Casting Notice: Hi, Innocent, you may be a match for the following roles." They will include the project name, type, union status, casting company with a role description, and a link to SUBMIT. Now, isn't that just amazing?

Some actors are a bit overwhelmed when faced with all these sites. Don't they all do the same thing, one might ask? Why are there so many different sites for submissions? It's all about opportunities! With all these tools, an actor can get their hustle on without waiting for anyone else. Don't have an agent? That's fine! Sign up for these sites and get some credits under your belt until you sign with someone. Once you take the time to set up these accounts properly, they will prove extremely useful. **You should never sit back and allow anyone to control your child's destiny in this acting business. Be proactive, know what's out there, and do your part to make it happen!**

STEP SEVEN

ECO CAST: IT IS HERE TO STAY

"PLEASE follow directions carefully, even if you think you already know what you're doing."

Although we touched on this previously, the "Eco Cast" phenomenon needs to be respected with an entire chapter. Eco Cast is a way for actors to submit "self-tapes." What is a self-tape? A self-tape is a virtual audition. This means you're taping yourself for the casting directors. Although it's been around for quite some time, this way of audition submissions grew in popularity when the entire world experienced a major 2-year shutdown. Actors either love submitting them or would rather eat peanut butter sandwiches for a week to avoid them. Allergic to peanuts? No problem. Make sure to have that emergency epinephrine pen handy, and they're good to go!

Seriously. I've heard from some actors that seeing the Eco Cast notification in their emails puts their stress and anxiety through the roof. For those living alone, the thought of self-tapes can be daunting. The actor must find a reader and ensure the lights, camera, and sound are up to par. Good luck if you live in a busy city and don't have an excellent noise-canceling panel or curtains. You can call a professional studio and book a 20-minute, 30-minute, or hour session, Reader included! Some studios even have virtual self-tape services where you are provided with the recording after your session. That's awesome! Still, some prefer the old-fashioned way of getting in the car and driving down to the casting office to give it a go. But with the rising price of gasoline, even those opposed to the notion of eco-casts can appreciate the convenience this system offers.

Allow me to be completely candid. Innocent's career soared during those years of lockdown. We took more time coaching each project, and he was able to send in the best representation of the character. (Yes, I'm his live-in acting coach as well. How did one little actor get to be so lucky!?) All those years of studying Meisner, Chekhov, and Stanislavski are paying off as I coach my son. I don't go in the room with him for in-person auditions, so I don't know how he's performing behind those closed doors. All I can do is sit in the waiting room and pray that he remembers most things from our coaching session and is utilizing his natural abilities to do his best. But being behind the camera to tweak little things gives me added confidence when submitting his self-tapes directly to Eco Cast or his representatives.

The self-tapes have become our calling card. Agents and managers can more confidently submit and pitch their young talent because they can see firsthand what the kids are capable of. With the necessity of Eco Cast, many agents and managers got an opportunity to experience their clients' acting like never before. After one self-tape submission, one of Innocent's reps told me that she had enjoyed watching him grow as an actor over the years. "Each time I get a self-tape, I'm excited to watch him. He's developed into an amazing actor," she said. They would not have been able to see his growth without watching scene after scene, character after character. This gave them even more confidence when submitting Innocent for more prominent roles because they knew firsthand that he possessed the skills to nail it.

When Innocent signed with a new agent, one of the first things they requested was a copy of recent self-tapes—both comedic and theatrical. And boy, did we have a field day with that! I have everything in the archive–feature films, episodic, comedy, drama, voice-over, singing, and dance. Those "shut-down" years helped us build an incredible arsenal of some of his best work. Even if he didn't book an audition, the work is still there, and it's still amazing.

HOW IT WORKS

Now, let's dig deeper into what a self-tape or Eco Cast request looks like. When an actor opens an email with the heading "You have an Eco Cast!" this can be very exciting. It's almost like a scavenger hunt—a new clue to the ultimate prize! It's an excellent opportunity to meet new casting directors, continue to impress the ones who already know your work, and ultimately book another significant role.

Although your representative initially submits your child for a role, you may receive an Eco Cast directly from your Actors Access account. You will receive a request to upload the audition tape by a specific time and date. Once the video is uploaded, the site will notify your representatives that the tape is ready for viewing. Once they have viewed and approved, the reps will officially hit the send/submit button on their end. Sometimes, you will be asked to submit directly to casting without the representative interface. This is one reason you will need to become very familiar with the process and know how to make the self-tape as professional as possible. Your child is not only representing themselves but also the agency or management company. Some receive private castings because of their reputation for having the highest quality of talent submissions. Ensure your child's self-tape is a positive notch in your rep's submission belt.

Back in the day, you would go into a casting director's office, do the scene maybe one or two times while they put you on tape, and then leave. With these self-tapes, you do the first step for the casting director. After the audition, they will edit and send the best takes to the next casting level. Generally, the director or producer decides if your child receives a callback. The CD calls you in initially because they see your photo and resume or you have a direct referral. They won't choose every tape that comes through to send to the director. They will select the best, which is why your child's self-tape must be professional and well-executed, following the casting director's instructions.

When your child is submitted for a role, and the casting director wants to see them on tape, you will receive an Eco Cast notice with instructions regarding the role and the audition. **PLEASE follow directions carefully, even if you think you already know what you're doing.** Missing a step, even one as simple as them asking you to include the slate at the end instead of the typical beginning, can cost you. Casting will provide a detailed description of how they would like the audition done (i.e., sitting, standing, no props, etc.). So, pay close attention to detail.

Casting offices have been great in assisting with this process as the dependence on this method is growing. Many provide tips on self-taping, or they will send you a link with the recommendations. How sweet is that?! They understand that self-tapes are new for many people and genuinely want you to succeed. I know many casting directors, and I have yet to meet one who wants to receive horrible self-tapes from actors. They want you to shine and be your best! It makes their job a whole lot easier. And which casting office wouldn't want to go down in history for discovering the next Brad Pitt or Angela Bassett?

EQUIPMENT

This is of the utmost importance. You will need to have your child stand in front of a neutral backdrop. No furniture or other items (unless the casting director requests them) should be present. Many actors have purchased a green, blue, gray, or beige screen to stand in front of while recording. I know adult actors who have painted a whole wall in their home a neutral color, so they don't have to go through the hassle of pulling out the backdrop screen for every audition. The background lets your child's performance stand out. You want the background as non-distracting as possible so your child will shine. The entire focus should be on them. For example, if a gorgeous white baby grand piano is in the background, the instrument may draw attention away from your child. Keep the background free and clear.

Light Source

The light source should be directly in front of your child. The video will look very dark if you position it behind them. Natural lighting is excellent, but your child must stand in front of the light source. Because we generally record our self-tapes against a wall in the bedroom, I have purchased different lighting systems to shine the best light on Innocent. We like the Softbox dimmable lights because they, like many others, come with multiple settings that can be brightened or dimmed. I recently purchased a clip-on light that can be attached to my cell phone, and I have found that when combined with my two studio lights, I can capture an even clearer picture. Whatever works best for you, ensure that there are limited to no shadows on your child's face due to inconsistent lighting. Also, my iPhone allows me to color correct any issues I might have with the original recording. When I start to edit Innocent's self-tape, I can make these corrections manually. With increasingly advanced technology, there are fewer chances of getting this wrong and more opportunities to impress!

Microphones

You don't need to purchase expensive microphones. I typically use our iPhone and turn the camera to selfie-video mode towards Innocent. Most updated iPhones have high-quality built-in mics that clearly pick up your voice. More important is ensuring you record in a quiet space for sound quality. I must admit that this has been a challenge for us. We tend to record many of our self-tapes at night because we live in a city, and you usually hear the traffic outside, especially during the daytime. I purchased a noise cancellation curtain, but that didn't work to my liking. Again, it's hit-and-miss. Whatever works for you is okay; make sure it's as quiet as possible. You can control air conditioning noises, television, and radios—make sure all of these devices are turned off to avoid their sound being picked up during the recording.

Tripod

This little tip may seem obvious, but it needs to be said. Make sure your camera does not move! Please do not take the camera in your hand and record your child. No matter how steady you think your hands are, casting can see the up-down-side-side movement from every subtle move. Please don't make them stop watching the audition because they're dizzy! Purchase a tripod stand to hold your camera so your hands can be free. You'll also need to have your hands free to hold the audition paper if you're the reader. And remember, your child is the one auditioning, not you. Casting generally stresses that the reader must NOT be seen on camera, and their voice should not overpower the one who is auditioning. This is their time to shine and show what they've got. You'll have your time later. Don't worry. Read with the appropriate enthusiasm and inflection so your child will have something to work off. Traditionally, actors have complained that they get thrown off when the reader lacks inflection. "They weren't giving me anything to work with!" Give your child "something to work with." Just don't be over-powering.

I went through the experience of an unsteady camera, which is why I know it can seem minute, but it is very important. There was an audition I wanted to record for Innocent quickly, and I didn't want to take the time to pull out the tripod and get it set up in the proper position. Yes, sometimes it takes some time to get it perfectly positioned. So, my brilliant self thought, *OK, no one will notice. Let me just hold the camera because it isn't that many lines. It'll be great, and we can get it to his manager quickly.* So, that's precisely what I did. When the manager saw the tape, she remarked what a fantastic audition Innocent gave but that I should try to keep the camera steady. Ahhhh, she could see those little movements??? Yes, everyone can see it—even the Casting Directors and the very near-sighted Mr. Magoo. We shot the audition over, and I took the time to do the work. Never skip a step, even when you don't feel like it.

Slate

During a self-tape, they will ask you to slate. A slate is an introduction of yourself and generally includes name, height, age (if your child is under 18), and loca-tion (the city where you live). Innocent can recite his slate in his sleep; he's done it so many times. The slate is necessary to identify your child to casting and anyone else who will be viewing the tape. If 50 actors submit videos, they need to know the actors' names to distinguish who they are and to identify them. They can't effectively say, "We liked the boy in the red jump-suit, suspenders, and cowboy boots." What if there were five boys with red jumpsuits, suspenders, and cowboy boots? I'm just saying … it could happen. The slate is generally at the beginning, but there are times when casting will ask you to put it at the end. Additionally, they may ask you to include a full-body shot and not a head-to-toe pan. This means they want to see their entire body shape at one time. You can achieve this by widening your camera angle and allowing the video to run for a few minutes. This will allow them enough time to get body type and height visual.

Wardrobe

There are differing opinions on this topic. Some believe that it doesn't matter what you wear, as long as the acting is good, and others think you should do your best to match the tone and personality of the character. I believe the latter. You do not have to go out and purchase expensive clothing for each audition. Use what you have in your child's closet. For example, Innocent had an audition to play a child lawyer, so I went through his closet and chose a good jacket and shirt, similar to what he might wear to church. Not only did it look great on camera, but it also helped him get into character. He's also had to audition for various sports roles, and I find shorts and tops to indi-

cate a sporty look. Since we can create a realistic character picture with these self-tapes, why not use them
to your full advantage? There used to be a saying in
Hollywood: *Show them what they're looking for.* So, if a
casting office is looking to cast a boy who can play
soccer, why not dress your child in clothing that looks
appropriate for the field? A picture is worth a thou-
sand words.

Keep in mind that there might be a time that you want
to go and purchase a specific wardrobe look, especially if there are casting requests. You know I'm
candid, so I'll tell you something that happened
recently. Innocent got an in-person audition for a
prominent national commercial that would require
exclusivity in a particular market for an extended
period. (Those are great commercials to book.) They
wanted the kids to dress like they were going to pee-
wee football practice. I googled what that looked like
and realized we had nothing in our closet to match the
look. So yes, this mom(ager) went to the store and
purchased an outfit that looked awesome and perfect
on my little one. He looked like a football player to
me!! Casting and the clients thought so as well. He
booked it. I'm not saying the wardrobe was the reason,
but it didn't hurt. They wanted to see a boy who
looked like he was practicing for pee wee football, so
that's exactly what we showed them.

Even though your camera will most likely be framed
from the chest upwards, there are many times a full

body slate is requested. If casting is looking to hire someone as a basketball player, showing their physique in shorts and a tank top gives an edge. I find that Innocent gets more in character when he's dressed similarly to the character. Once, he was asked to audition for a boy about to go to bed, so he opted to wear pajamas. He nailed the audition because he embodied the feel of a kid getting comfy before bedtime. Even if the casting director doesn't see the pajama bottoms, what is essential is that it helps my son get into character. Now, this isn't for everyone. Whatever is best for your child to deliver the most genuine audition, you can try it. And let your kids have some input, also. Sometimes I've told Innocent to put on a pair of jeans and a t-shirt, and let's shoot this thing, honey! But he's quick to note that the role doesn't *feel* right in that clothing, and he will suggest an alternate outfit that allows him to feel closer to the character. If it follows the self-tape dos and don'ts in terms of wardrobe, I allow him to explore his choices. After all, he's the one in front of the camera!

COACHING

As mentioned before, I am Innocent's coach, and we always coach for each role. I have friends with no clue about acting, so they usually have a coach on hand for significant roles. These coaching sessions can take place over Zoom, so there's no excuse not to take advantage. If you're not an actor or don't understand the process of acting, please put in as much effort as possible to give your child the best chance for a booking. Even if they don't book that particular role, the casting director will remember them for future projects. A group of casting directors repeatedly call my son in for various projects. It's not because he books every project for them, but because they know his work. They appreciate that he delivers professional self-tapes and excellent acting skills (patting Coach Mama on the back).

REMEMBER

Self-tapes can be the first impression a casting director has of your child if this is the first time they are calling them in for an audition. First impressions are lasting. They can make or break. You want this impression to show your child in their most fantastic light. It's best practice to ensure instructions are followed to a tee. The lighting is on point, the sound is good, your child looks great on camera, and you have done the work to either coach them or have them professionally coached for the role.

Overall, we love the self-tape process. Even Innocent enjoys it. It allows him to be seen by casting directors worldwide and to book jobs that are not solely based in Los Angeles, where we live. His first starring role in Apple TV's *Little America* was booked from a self-tape. The callback included the casting director and director—all on Zoom. He nailed it, and we were packing our bags a few weeks later to go to New York/New Jersey for two weeks. The 2nd significant role also came from self-tapes ... the long-awaited *Ivy + Bean* films! YAY! The callback was also via Zoom with the director and casting director. The chemistry read audition (which lasted about 2 hours) was also via Zoom. The chemistry read is where they pair actors to see the chemistry they have together, side by side. Traditionally, this is done in person. Still, the pandemic allowed a new unique trend to connect actors from across the globe! A few weeks after that Zoom chemistry read, we packed our bags and headed to Vancouver, British Columbia, for the next three months. Embrace the self-tape process. Enjoy it. Get good at it. Use them as an advantage because they will be around for a long time.

The submission process begins when you sign your child up on the casting sites. You must be ready for what comes next. One thing that can trip you up is not planning for the next steps. The industry won't wait for you to learn. Parents I've assisted with the process of landing representation were prepared and knew exactly what to do when asked to self-tape a week after signing with an agent. Why? Because I had already briefed them on this process. They felt more confident and didn't have to go back to ask the agent for assistance. If your child signs with an agent today, and their agent sends an Eco Cast tomorrow due by 3 pm the next day, what do you do? Can you take a crash course on how to do everything? Only if you want to completely stress yourself out and remove the joy from the process for your child. If you're reading this book before you begin the process, BRAVO!!! You're ahead of the game.

STEP EIGHT

THE CASTING TEAM: PUTTING IT ALL TOGETHER

"In the Acting Business, RELATIONSHIP is Key."

Navigating the acting business requires a well-oiled team of players working together to get your child BOOKED. It is essential to understand the role everyone plays and what you must do to develop positive relationships with this cast of players. Before I get into this Step's chicken and waffles, a straightforward key to success is keeping a detailed log. Keep track of your child's auditions, casting directors, directors, and producers. If you're just starting as the parent of a Showbiz Kid, perfect ... you can start now. If you're already the parent of a Showbiz Kid, perfect ... you can still start now. It's never too late or too early to start. This list will prove helpful as your child continues in the industry. Because everything is built on these relationships, it is essential to remember the people you meet and interact with. You may notice they start getting repeat calls and contacts from the same people. You need to know who these people are and express appreciation for their repeated interactions with your child whenever possible!

When I first arrived in Los Angeles a couple of moons ago, there were notable casting directors who would continue to bring me in repeatedly. At the time, I didn't realize the true importance and blessing of this. When you have a casting director rooting for you, they will keep you in mind for projects that come across their desk for which your child may be suitable. It's crucial to encourage your child always to do their best for each audition. Even if you look at the character and think, *there's no way they will pick my child because the character is six, and my child is ten.* Whatever the reason, let your ten-year-old knock out their best version of a six-year-old. Even if they don't get cast, the casting director will surely remember their dynamic portrayal. It's not always the booking that gets you called back; sometimes, it's the consistent, amazing work your child does.

CASTING DIRECTORS

Contrary to what some actors may believe, casting directors *want* you to succeed. It gives them an excellent reputation for bringing in quality talent. Every time they push play on a self-tape or watch an in-person audition, they hope they will be blown away by your child's choices and talent. They saw a special "something" that caused them to bring your child in for the audition in the first place. I think this is one thing my son truly gets. He knows his parents want him to succeed at everything he does. He knows his parents are rooting for him every time he gets in front of the camera. I encourage him to imagine that same encouragement coming from the casting directors or anyone watching his tape. "Innocent, do you know they want you to succeed just as much as we do?" When he truly gets that through his head, he can bring more of an authentic quality to the table because he doesn't begin from a place of self-defeat.

I've had adult actors call me after auditions, and I'll ask how it went. "Oh, they looked at me funny when I was in the waiting room. I could feel they didn't like me from the beginning." Really? And you think you'll go into a room and nail it with *that* attitude? So much of the audition process is mind over matter! Speak positively into your life because if you don't, who will?

Remember, casting directors are human too, and everyone enjoys encouragement. One CD who requests my son frequently for auditions also called me in for many auditions even before Innocent was born. Recently, I went in for an audition, and I took a moment to thank them for calling Innocent in. He frequently books with their casting office. In another instance, I was at an in-person audition with my son, and the names sounded very familiar. I quickly searched in my email and realized they were the same CDs that had cast Innocent in another national commercial. When I got a moment to speak with the casting associate, I thanked her for booking Innocent on that project. She was happy for the acknowledgment and said she would inform the head of casting that their office had booked him for a national campaign the prior year.

In the acting business, relationship is key. Talent is crucial, but there's another element that actors are quick to admit, even though it may not seem fair. Having and maintaining the right connections is closely linked to success. No, life is not always fair, and *Showbizness* is life. Like anything else we deal with, you must learn (and teach your child) to navigate this world and use it to your advantage. All actors know that you must fight for that booking. With that in mind, get all the training necessary for the "knockout."

THE KNOCKOUT PROCESS

Round 1: Casting Director

Production puts out a breakdown for the role of an African American / Multi-ethnic female aged 6-8 to play the role of Will Smith's daughter in his upcoming feature. They have chosen "Awesome Casting" to cast their project. The role description comes out on the

Breakdowns, and agents and managers quickly submit their clients who fit the description. The first thing that will grab their attention is the headshot. Casting directors will have to sift through many submissions to select the actresses they will interview for the audition. Every agent and manager can send in their top choices if the casting agency has made a public breakdown submission. (If they do not publish the breakdown, they will send it to a few agents and managers they know will submit their top talent.) They have published the breakdown for this case and may choose 20 actresses to audition (in person or via self-tape). Your child is selected in this first round. You submit a self-tape, and the casting directors love her initial audition and send the tape to the client (producers and director) for review. They now need to choose a smaller group of girls and narrow the selections further.

Round 2: The Callback

Your child did well enough in the 1st round that the casting director asks to see them again, generally per the client's request. Round 2 is the callback; they are calling you back for the 2nd time. The callback is used to narrow down the pool so that the casting director is submitting top talent they feel will impress the producers, writers, or directors. The callback can be in person or virtually. If virtually, you will be given a time with a Zoom link (or similar) to sign in and wait until you are called to be seen. During the callback, the

CD may have your child reread the scenes and engage in conversation to get to know them better. During this session, the Casting director or assistant will act as the reader.

Round 3: Producers Session

Your child did well in the callback, and the CD and client are confident that they could envision your child in the role of Will Smith's daughter. They are eager to bring your child to other producers and network decision makers to get their take. In this session, the producers will be in the room. Your child should do the same thing she did in the callback and wear the same clothing and hairstyle if possible. This is not the time to change anything. They liked what they saw initially, so give them that again unless they request otherwise. Getting to the producer's session is a big deal!

Round 4: The Booking

Contrary to what some may think, casting directors don't usually make the final decision. They bring actors in front of those responsible for making the final decision. Once they get the final approval, they call you and give you the official booking. For TV, the executive producer may be the ultimate decision-maker after collaborating with the other executive team members. There may be multiple directors in the series. Many times, there is a different director per episode. In Film, the director will have the final say because it's geared more toward the director's vision.

Whoever makes the decision must ensure your child shows their best skills and personality to all involved. The industry, as I said, is like a big family. Even if your child doesn't get the job of Will Smith's daughter, you had better believe the casting director will continue to call on her for other projects. Again, this was a standard example of how it works and can differ from project to project. In *Showbiz*, nothing is set in stone, as shown in the following real-life examples.

REAL LIFE

Little America

Innocent booked one of the lead roles in *Little America* on Apple TV. Here is a brief timeline of how this happened:

- The self-tape came in on 4/17/19 at 3:57 pm and was due back by 4/18/19 at 3 pm.
- I turned the self-tape in on 4/17/19 at 10:53 pm.
- On 4/18/19, the casting director set a time to meet Innocent for a virtual callback the next day.
- On 4/19/19 at 1:45 pm, the casting director and the director are on the call. With the casting director reading, Innocent had to

recreate the scenes. I remember we weren't familiar with the whole Zoom thing, and I was sweating as I tried to keep him still in front of the camera while I held it. (I hadn't purchased a tripod yet because there wasn't a need for them yet.)

- On 4/19/19 at 7:52 pm, Innocent's agent emailed, "INNOCENT GOT THE OFFER! YAAAY! CONGRATULATIONS!" It was one of the most exciting days in his career.

Ivy + Bean

Here is yet another example of how quickly this process works.

- On 5/5/21, Innocent received a notice from his agent for a self-tape for *Ivy + Bean*. It was due 5/7/21 by 3 pm.
- I sent his audition tape in on 5/6/21. (We like to be early and not wait until the last minute!)
- On 5/10/21, the agent informed us there would be director's sessions and to stay tuned for more info.
- On 5/11/21, the agent set the callback for the next day.
- On 5/12/21 at 4:30 pm, the callback went well. That same day they sent out a notice that Innocent had been invited for a chemistry

read so he could interact with the other kids and assess their chemistry.

- The chemistry read was held on 5/13/21. It was a virtual session that lasted approximately 2 hours.
- On 5/18/21, I got a 2-way call from BOTH the manager and the agent. *Mmmm, now that was unusual.* I braced myself. I knew something was up. Innocent had just booked the supporting role of Leo in the Netflix film trilogy *Ivy+ Bean*!!!!! We were heading to Vancouver, British Columbia, Canada, for three months a few weeks later!

I get chills as I write this even now. It was such a life-changing event. I heard later that they auditioned thousands of children worldwide to land the roles. When I received a call from Vancouver to arrange Innocent's education on set, I was told, "So, I heard they found their Leo in Los Angeles! The search has been a big one." I was so proud! I would never have imagined the joy we're able to feel as parents when our kids do well in this life. It's literally on a whole other level.

Both examples illustrate what goes into the booking process and how they can vary from show to show. Again, there is no hard or fast rule. Stay ready, so you don't have to get ready. Flexibility is key. When your child gets to a certain point in their career, some tough decisions will need to be made. Do I regret giving up my singing gig in Africa to fly to New York with Innocent and shoot *Little America* for two weeks in New York/New Jersey? ABSOLUTELY NOT. Now, it's not for everyone to sacrifice at this level for their child. If Innocent were older, I could have had someone else accompany him. Still, I knew my little man needed his acting-coach-momager-and-mama on set with him to succeed and tuck him in bed at night with dozens of kisses and cuddles. That way, he could present the best version of himself possible. Was I sad that I didn't get to go and sing in Africa again and showcase my talents? Of course! But even the client, who had kids, told me that she understood the choice I had to make. Although they would miss me singing at their event, they said, "Innocent comes first, and this may be the project that starts an even bigger career for him." I was humbled and touched by their under-standing because some people will NOT understand, and you have to be ok with that. I believe I listened to Whitney Houston's song a couple of times to encourage me during that period: "I believe the chil-dren are our future. Teach them well and let them lead the way. Show them all the beauty they possess inside. Give them a sense of pride to make it easier. Let the children's laughter remind us how we used to be." Cue happy tears…

From the private car service, beautiful 5-star hotel, comfortable honey wagon on set, and special bonds formed with his co-stars and directors—it was priceless. My son learned many valuable lessons that set a precedence for him at a very young age and showed him what's possible to achieve. I remind him whenever I can, "Baby, with GOD, ALL things are possible." And he truly believes that.

THE HUSTLE AND GRIND

IT'S ALL WORTH IT

"It takes a village for your child to succeed in this industry, as it does with anything."

P arents or guardians, I commend you for taking the time to research and ensure your little one has the best opportunity for success. If you're reading this book now, know this: Kids need an adult to help them navigate this industry. In Innocent's case, he couldn't even read when he first started, so I had to "feed him the lines" until he memorized them. That's exactly how he landed his first starring role at age five. I remember thinking, *Boy, I can't wait until you can read your own scripts! It'll take some of the pressure off me!* But seriously, I'm so proud of everyone out there. **It takes a village for your child to succeed in this industry, as it does with anything.**

To all the momagers and popagers out there, know that the hustle and grind you put in today is worth it, especially if your child has a passion for this industry. It's not an easy job, but somebody's got to do it: answering emails, recording and editing self-tapes, following up with representation, putting together wardrobe, helping memorize lines, coaching for auditions, keeping work permits up to date, setting up Coogan accounts, going on set as your child's high-end personal assistant, sending agents and managers periodic holiday and birthday gifts, sending thank you notes, and even sacrificing some parts of your career. All of this takes the greatest love, courage, and dedication. Even if you don't hear it often, THANK YOU!!! Everyone connected to the industry appreciates parents and guardians like you because working with child actors would be impossible without you.

If you ever feel overwhelmed by the pressure and fast pace of the industry, it's OK to take a little break. You can send your agent or manager "book out dates" for your child, which means you won't be available to receive auditions during that period. When we travel out of state, for example, I send "physical book out dates" but let them know we are still available for all virtual castings during that period. Now, if we go on a cruise or something like that (Believe God with me, fam!), I'll send out complete book-out dates for that time frame. That means don't call or email me because I'll be having too much fun to even look at my phone! I can give my mind a rest from all of the hustle and bustle. Sometimes that is necessary. If you or your child starts to feel burned out or overwhelmed, it's perfectly cool to do a "staycation" for a few days and book out. Employees have allotted vacation days and sick days even on regular jobs. Don't feel guilty for doing this. Your agent or manager won't hold it against you because even they take their vacations!!!

Now that you've read this book from cover to cover, I hope you feel even more encouraged and equipped to help build your child's career. If you're just starting, excellent! You can go back through some of these chapters and use them step by step as you navigate this world. This is precisely what I do with the parents I assist through this journey. Take deep breaths, go step by step, and learn as much as possible about the process. If you don't, it is easy to feel completely overwhelmed. Sometimes, I use a treasure hunt approach. When working with young actors and their parents, I may not give them the entire picture at once. Once they find and complete the first task I've assigned, they get clues to complete the next. If I give them all the clues at once, they might get confused or wildly ambitious and skip steps, which can take them right back to square one.

If you're already a pro, wonderful! You can use this as a refresher or for those few little things you may not be sure about. You can also take some of my personal experiences to validate what you're going through right now, and we can simply breathe together and know we're not alone.

Whichever position you're in, enjoy the journey. Don't get anxious; don't over-stress yourself. Know that everything will happen at the perfect time for your child. Once you complete an audition, let it go. Don't let your worry and insecurity cause the same feelings for your child. Not until Innocent was older did he start asking me, "Did I get the part?" And that's usually when he gets auditions for a Nickelodeon or Disney show he watches regularly. Other than that, he won't even ask me. Once, we were on our way to a commercial job, and he asked, "Are we going for the audition?"

I said, "Baby, we're going to the job."

"Oh, I booked it?" he asked casually. "Cool."

I loved it! I said to myself, *Yes! I've done something right as a parent.* Blending the momager and mom hats requires a delicate balance essential for your child's ultimate success and longevity in this industry.

I can't wait to hear all of your amazing testimonies after you finish these last few sentences. Let's keep in touch, fam. Join me on Facebook (ShowbizKidsInc), Instagram (ShowbizFam), YouTube (ShowbizFam), or on our website, www.Showbiz-Kids.com. And please, spread the love and knowledge by heading to Amazon or whichever platform you partnered with to seek this knowledge. Your review could be the one that helps a prospective or current parent or guardian decide to go all-in to help take their child's dreams to the next level. From the bottom of my heart, Innocent's mama thanks you so much! Now, let's get out there and get busy, Showbiz fam!!! Our kids are counting on us.

★★★★★

Showbiz Kids

We're giving you 5-Stars for reading this book! We would truly appreciate it if you would take just 60 seconds to write a brief review on Amazon. Feel free to take a screenshot of your favorite section and add it to the review! And don't forget to download the **Showbiz Kids 8 Steps Organizer** to keep track of all your WINS!
www.Showbiz-Kids.com

Much Success, Showbiz Kids

Visit the link below or scan the QR Code to leave a Review

https://www.amazon.com/review/create-review/? channel=glance-detail&ie=UTF8&asin= B0BG5CM89D

LEAVE A QUICK REVIEW!

★★★★★

Showbiz Kids

We're giving you 5-Stars for reading this book!
We would truly appreciate it if you would take
just 60 seconds to write a brief review on
Amazon. Feel free to take a screenshot of your
favorite section and add it to the review! And
don't forget to download the
Showbiz Kids 8 Steps Organizer to keep track
of all of your WINS!

Much Success, Showbiz Kids

<<<Click Here to leave a quick Review

www.Showbiz-Kids.com

To leave a quick review just scan the QR code below!

SHOWBIZ KIDS
8 STEPS ORGANIZER

A FREE GIFT TO OUR READERS
DOWNLOAD AT WWW.SHOWBIZ-KIDS.COM

RESOURCES

Actors Access—Login. (n.d.). Actors Access. https://actorsaccess. com/actor/?view=welcomeCastingNetworks.com

ARTICLE 5.5. Independent Study [51744—51749.6]. (1976). California Legislative Information. https://leginfo.legislature.ca.gov/ faces/codes_displaySection.xhtml?sectionNum=51745.& lawCode=EDC

ARTICLE 6. Duties of Employer [49160—49165]. (1976). California Legislative Information. https://leginfo.legislature.ca.gov/ faces/codes_displaySection.xhtml?sectionNum=49160.& lawCode=EDC

Auditions & Casting Calls | casting talent. (n.d.). Casting Frontier. https://castingfrontier.com/

CHAPTER 2. Occupational Privileges and Restrictions [1285—1312]. (1937). California Legislative Information. https://leginfo.legis lature.ca.gov/faces/codes_displaySection.xhtml?sectionNum= 1308.5.&lawCode=LAB

CHAPTER 3. Contracts in Art, Entertainment, and Professional Sports [6750—6753]. (1992). California Legislative Information. https://leginfo.legislature.ca.gov/faces/codes_displaySection. xhtml?sectionNum=6753.&lawCode=FAM

Gobbell, M. (2020, August 22). What are normal attention spans for children? *The Kid's Directory Family Resource Guide.* https:// www.kids-houston.com/2020/08/21/what-are-normal-atten tion-spans-for-children/

Information on minors and employment. (n.d.). California.Gov; State of California Department of Industrial Relations. https://www. dir.ca.gov/dlse/dlse-cl.htm

Jackie. (2022). In *Wikipedia.* https://en.wikipedia.org/w/index. php?title=Jackie&oldid=1099043942

Jackie Coogan. (2022). In *Wikipedia.* https://en.wikipedia.org/w/ index.php?title=Jackie_Coogan&oldid=1102181309

Masser, M. (1985). *Greatest Love of All* [Recorded by W. Houston].

MinorsContracts.com. (n.d.). https://sites.google.com/site/ minorscontracts/

Robinson, D. (1985). *Chaplin, his life and art* (1st McGraw-Hill ed). McGraw-Hill.

Terry, J. R. (2018). The wolf at the door: Child actors in liminal legal spaces. *The Journal of the History of Childhood and Youth, 11*(1), 57–62. https://doi.org/10.1353/hcy.2018.0005

The Kid's Directory. (n.d.). The Kid's Directory Family Resource Guide. https://www.kids-houston.com/

(N.d.). SAG-AFTRA. https://www.sagaftra.org/